'Delightful ... [Hill] potently evokes th............. ... ...

musicians she knows or knew are vividly sketched ... a richly idiosyncratic memoir of a bibliophile. Best of all, it ignites a passion for books one hasn't read, or even thought of.' *Mail on Sunday*

'This thought-provoking book gives both inspiration on new titles to explore and a soothing sense that reading is indeed a vital and central part of living.' *Press Association*

'Hill is wise, affectionate, insightful. Here is a distillation of a lifetime of reading, writing, editing, publishing, buying, hoarding, lending, borrowing and dog-earing books.' *The Times*

'The bookworm in your life will be champing at the bit to read [Hill's] recommendations' *Saga*

SUSAN HILL is the winner of numerous literary prizes, including the Somerset Maugham award. In 2014, she was awarded a CBE for her services to literature. Her books have won awards and prizes including the Whitbread and the John Llewellyn Rhys and the Somerset Maugham; and have been shortlisted for the Booker. Author of the Simon Serrailler crime series and numerous other novels, her previous literary memoir, Howards End is on the Landing, and the ghost stories *The Small Hand, The Travelling Bag* and *Printers Devil Court* are all published by Profile. *The Woman in Black*, which has been running in the West End for thirty years, and was a h............................rdback.

Jacob's Room Is Full of Books

Susan Hill

PROFILE BOOKS

This paperback edition published in 2018

First published in Great Britain in 2017 by
PROFILE BOOKS LTD
3 Holford Yard
Bevin Way
London
WC1X 9HD
www.profilebooks.com

1 3 5 7 9 10 8 6 4 2

Typeset in Transitional by MacGuru Ltd
Printed and bound in Great Britain by
CPI Group (UK) Ltd, Croydon CR0 4YY

ISBN 978 1 78125 081 5
eISBN 978 1 84765 919 4

Mixed Sources
Product group from well-managed
forests and other controlled sources
www.fsc.org Cert no. TT-COC-002227
© 1996 Forest Stewardship Council
FSC

For my friend Lynne Hatwell

aka *Dove Grey Reader*

Who has read more books than me – and she's younger

JANUARY

NEW YEAR NON-WEATHER. Wet. Dank. Grey. Chilly but not winter cold.

And people have made me cross. I have never 'done' New Year. Time is seamless. Months, days, weeks, years are artificial, manmade things, so what are we celebrating? Personal choice, of course, and I don't in the least mind retiring to bed at ten p.m. with a good book and hearing the fireworks exploding all round me a couple of hours later. But going out this morning, by the ford – that beautiful, healing spot where the river runs shallow and clear over grey stones and one sees kingfishers – just there, fireworks have been let off on the grassy bank, and all the detritus of cardboard tubes and wooden sticks and burnt-out plastic has been left where it has fallen. Never mind that nobody bothered to pick anything up – they probably didn't even notice. None of it looks very bio-degradable.

I am not a loud fusser-about-litter. I know I ought to join picking-up parties but somehow I never do. But, like discarded plastic hamburger boxes and Coke cans, the firework mess is a mess too far.

━●◦●━

I FIND A LADYBIRD, living on my bedside table. I could do with some decoration, the house looks so bare after Christmas. Is this the only insect absolutely everybody loves? Would we find it so charming if it had, say, a sludge green back instead of a scarlet patent leather one? Is it the spots that do it? What if it were transparent?

Now, a Red Admiral butterfly has emerged from some crevice and is fluttering round the room, having come in on the logs and hatched in the warmth. It pats the windowpane softly. But it is far better off staying inside. It is light and warm in here and it might live for days. If I let it out into the bitterly cold night, it will die in minutes.

Vladimir Nabokov was a butterfly expert. If an author's full biography is not generally of interest in separation from the work, sometimes the odd incongruous fact may amuse us and add an extra dimension to the writing as well. Nabokov was a world-renowned lepidopterist. T. S. Eliot worked for years in a bank. Both those facts seem exactly right.

And Noel Coward spent his last weeks reading E. Nesbit. *The Story of the Treasure Seekers. Five Children and It. The Railway Children.*

Who knew?

———•○•———

Freezing wet December, then …
Bloody January again!

I ALWAYS THINK that's by Joyce Grenfell, until I check and as usual find that it is by Flanders and Swann. Theirs was the sort of humour beloved of old-fashioned vicars and their wives. They roared at 'Mud, mud, glorious mud', they hooted at 'And 'twas on a Monday morning that the gas man came to call'. They rocked at 'I'm a gnu' and when the line (after a pause) 'A GN-OTHER GNU' came, they laughed until their sides ached and the tears ran down their cheeks. Vicarly humour is very simple. Flanders and Swann, with their impeccable timing and songs that brought the small struggles of everyday domestic life into focus, were a great partnership. But they haven't really stood the test and taste of time, though 'I once had a whim, and I had to obey it/To buy a French horn in a second-hand shop' – sung to the tune of Mozart's Horn Concerto – is still delightfully entertaining.

Massed clergy loved Joyce Grenfell, too. So did I. But have her slightly arch, slightly coy way of singing and doing monologues dated, too? Quite a few of them have, but 'Old Girls' School Reunion' comes up fresh every time you hear it, because it is still so true – or it has been in my experience. 'Ah, Ma'mselle … c'est très gentil de vous voir,' spoken in the perfect Franglais accent. 'Remember me? Lumpy Latimer.'

She brought that, and so many other light-hearted pieces, to vivid life because there was a touch of the old girl about Joyce herself. The fact that she was a little goofy meant that she could play a police sergeant posing as a games mistress in the wondrous film *The Belles of St Trinian's*, wearing a panama hat and brandishing a hockey stick, to perfection.

Her one-woman shows, *Joyce Grenfell Requests the Pleasure* and several others, in which she always had some amusing friends as guests, were hugely popular with the middle-aged and elderly middle classes and, of course, the vicars. She took people off and she poked gentle fun, but there was not a breath of malice in them.

I can sing 'Stately as a Galleon' from beginning to end. I wonder how many others are left who can do that. But Joyce Grenfell is perhaps best remembered for her infant school teacher monologue – all infant school teachers sound like her – in which she utters the immortal, perfectly inflected line, 'George … Don't do that.'

Happy days, when vicars and the rest were satisfied by such innocent, simple pleasures as Flanders and Swann and Joyce Grenfell. Satire, The Establishment club, *That Was The Week That Was* and the black humour songs of Tom Lehrer were the beginning of the end for all that.

DARK WALK UP THE LANE, with dog, cat and torch. Two tawny owls fly up in alarm from the oak trees. A bit further on, one barn owl silently glides from the field. There is a whole world out there living its own life without reference to us.

It is often said that mankind needs a faith if the world is to be improved. In fact, unless the faith is vigilantly and regularly checked by a sense of man's fallibility it is likely to make the world worse. From Torquemada to Robespierre and Hitler, the men who have made mankind suffer the most have been inspired to do so by a strong faith – so strong that it led them to think their crimes were acts of virtue, necessary to help them achieve their aim, which was to build some sort of ideal kingdom on earth.

But, as we have been told on very good authority, the Kingdom of Heaven is not of this world. Those who think they can establish it here are more likely to create a hell on earth.

I found this, written down on a piece of paper inside a file. It's from David Cecil's *Library Looking-Glass* and seems entirely true and pertinent.

WHEN I WAS SEVEN, I got pocket money for the first time – not a lot, but enough to buy my weekly copy of the *Beano*, so I was happy. When my daughter Jess was the same age, she got enough to buy some penny sweets every Saturday – and her copy of the *Beano*. The routine was always the same. She settled back in the big, reclining armchair. She lined her sweets up carefully along the arms, in order of eating. And then she reclined and opened her comic. Once, as she did so, I heard her sigh, 'Ahhhhh. This is the life, readers.'

Now, at roughly the same age, my step-great-nephew, Ollie, has just been given an annual subscription to the *Beano* for Christmas.

What is it about comics? Why did the parents of my generation of children so disapprove of them? Maybe some still do, but not many, because now we have graphic books – sometimes original, sometimes re-tellings of Shakespeare and other classics – and they seem quite acceptable.

I can't read anything in strip form now, or at least nothing longer than the Snipcock & Tweed cartoon in *Private Eye*, but somehow I can still manage the *Beano Annual*, which I am given every year.

Was it the anarchic, subversive element of the Bash Street Kids and other low-life of which our parents so disapproved? Was it all the joyous KERPOW!!!!! SPLAT!!! and ZOOOOOOM!!!!! which emboldened the pages? A bit of both and more, I suspect. But I think a mild form of anarchy should prevail among the under-tens. Via the *Beano* and the like, they see that kids can mock and deride and misbehave and cause mayhem and still survive and thrive, and that AUTHORITY does not always have the last word. It is all good old-fashioned fun. I sometimes wonder what Ollie makes of teachers wearing mortarboards, though.

I once interviewed a representative from the *Beano*'s publisher, D. C. Thompson, on a Radio 4 book programme. It was harder to get hold of him than someone from MI5. They're a cunning lot up there in Dundee, they play their comic cards very close to their chests. But after extracting drops of blood from the Scots stone, I got him to reveal that they were creating a new character, to go alongside Gnasher. Now, this had involved two years or more of market surveys, creative conferences, design meetings and Lord knows what else. A new character is a Big Deal in the comic world and it can't be seen to fail. It has to stand the test of the next twenty-five years of readers – at least.

But finally, finally, they had come up with Gnasher's little brother, Gnipper. And the man from the *Beano* said, 'Because he goes gnip, gnip, gnip.' And he emitted a Dundee-an chuckle and with that chuckle, which was only a tad short of gleeful, I realised that the grown-up men who create the *Beano* weekly for their paid work are just a bunch of 9-year-old boys. It was very heartening.

SPENDING A QUIET WEEK working in a rented Cotswold cottage. As usual, there are books on the shelves left behind by previous renters and here is *Embers* by the Hungarian writer Sandor Marai, one of those books that sprang fully formed out of Zeus's head to become, when it was re-published in English a few years ago, the novel everyone was reading. Publishers call them 'word of mouth' books but they are more – they are word of the internet, the online book groups, the seen-a-fellow-commuter-reading-it books. John Williams' *Stoner* was another such. Josephine Hart sent me a copy one Christmas – I had never heard of it and nor had many other people, but she was the kind of generous book-lover who just bought fifty copies of something she liked and sent them to friends. That is enough to start a ball rolling, but only if all other things are equal – meaning, not only must said book be exceptionally good, but it must have the X factor which makes it appeal to a wide variety of readers, crossing sexes, ages, reading types. *Stoner* did that. It had a universal appeal. So did *Embers*. All manner of people loved them both, not just those who prefer crime fiction, or love stories, or sagas, or books in translation, or very literary fiction, or books about animals, or historical novels, or … The formula for word-of-mouth bestsellers is a mystery. Everyone wants it, everyone would like to bottle it. Nobody ever has and when they try, they are always doomed to fail and get their fingers burned.

I pick up *Embers* to read again and, after a few chapters, realise that the same thing could happen to this a second time. It is a beautiful novel. It has lost none of its attraction, it has not 'dated' or been done again but better. Indeed, I think that is one of the tests of this sort of book – that it is a one-off. It is not 'If you liked this you will enjoy that …' It is just itself. There are as many novels about love as there are pebbles on a beach. But how many are there about friendship? Yes, friendship is a form of love, but I mean in its purest, simplest form – friendship. I can think of some children's books about friendship – Tove Jansson's Finn

Family Moomintroll series, for a start. There are many about friendship between a human and an animal, too. But friendship as friendship?

Sometimes, one short paragraph can reveal that you have in your hands a novel by a great writer:

> *It is the kind of idea that comes later to most people. Decades pass,*
> *one walks through a darkened room in which someone has died, and*
> *suddenly one recalls long forgotten words and the roar of the sea.*
> (Embers)

The message, if not the rule, is always to leave behind on the shelves the books you have enjoyed yourself when on holiday, for someone else to find. Perhaps that's another way a slow-burner overtakes the pack to become a bestseller.

———•◦•———

I HAD A KINDLE. I read books on it for maybe six months, and then I stopped and went back to printed books. I did not do it for any reasons whatsoever other than organic ones. I prefer holding a real book, turning paper pages over, turning them back, bending the spine, dog-earing the corners, underlining in pencil, making margin notes in pen. My taste. I can see all of the arguments for the convenience of the e-reader but I like to have a physical relationship with my books.

There is more, though. I gave up reading on a Kindle because I found I was not taking the words and their meaning in, as I do those in a printed book. They went in through my eyes but seemed to glide off into some underworld, without touching my brain, memory or imagination, let alone making any permanent mark there. I was puzzled by this, until I learned that if we use an e-reader or a laptop before going to sleep, our brains are affected so that we are more likely to sleep badly. It is something to do with the blue light. I've forgotten. The e-reader is cold, and what I mean by that I cannot put into words or explain, I can only feel that it is the right way of describing the experience, as against the warmth of a physical book.

Cold room, warm bed, good book. But I think whatever this blue light thing is, it is responsible for making the printed word slide past the brain on its way to oblivion.

I do not travel much and never go on long-haul flights. Friends who do, popping over to New Zealand as I might pop over the road, can take a dozen, or a hundred, long tomes loaded on to one small, light e-reader. And I can see the charm and convenience of that. Even if they never sleep and return home with no memory whatsoever of what they have read.

●•○•●

IS LISTENING TO an audio book the same as reading it? In the most obvious sense, no. I don't listen to them myself. I prefer to read in silence, and to be able to go back and over a paragraph again. I want to hear the voice of a narrator sound as I imagine them to sound. But if I were blind, of course I would listen to them. My great uncle Leonard, who had been blind since he was fourteen, had Books for the Blind delivered to him every other week. They were heavy leather boxes containing large, cumbersome records and his pleasure in listening to Churchill's war-time speeches, or J. B. Priestley reading his own essays, was very great.

He sat in his armchair of an evening, fingers making a steeple in front of his face, and listened for two or three hours. My great aunt took him a cup of tea and a biscuit at half time, and at ten o'clock he went to bed. I had gone to my own several hours before, of course, but I lay listening for as long as I could possibly stay awake, hearing the growl of Winston Churchill intoning through the wall. The books were provided free and delivered and collected free, courtesy of Libraries for the Blind. It was a lifeline.

Now, people cycling and running, ironing and train travelling, appear to be listening to audio books through headphones – though I am sure more of them listen to pop music – and the crime writer Val McDermid listens to them all the time while she is pounding a treadmill. But, for me, listening still loses out to the reader's silent progress along the lines, and so down the sentences, the paragraphs. I also find that the reader's voice gets in the way, or it is a voice I don't like, or worse, find seriously grating. But audio books are selling as never before, so I must be wrong. No, not wrong. Just different. Besides, most sighted people I know who sometimes listen to audio books also read books to themselves.

The BBC gave us some iconic readings of famous books. Whoever chose Martin Jarvis to read the *Just William* books, and Alan Bennett to read *Winnie the Pooh*, was a casting genius. Ah, *Just William*. So many adults listened to those readings on Radio 4. So many of us remember William, his mate Ginger, his sister Ethel and her soppy fiancé Robert, and the dreadful Violet Elizabeth Bott, who would thcream and thcream until she was thick. A friend's daughter recently called her new baby Violet Elizabeth. She had no idea …

■●●●■

MEANWHILE, THE TEMPERATURE has dropped to minus 7, the fire is lit and I am re-reading May Sarton's *Journal of a Solitude*. I have never known such a self-regarding, self-indulgent author. Yet isn't writing a journal bound to be an outpouring of self? No. I can think of so many diaries and journals that of course are about the writer and her or his life and experiences, feelings, thoughts, beliefs, friends … but which do not seem self-centred in this way. May Sarton was, by all accounts including her own, the most infuriating woman to know. She believed she was a major poet, that poetry was her form. She was wrong. She thought she was a fine novelist. She was an OK one. How harsh this is. But she is dead and cannot read me.

She was a woman tormented by her own temperament, by her rages, storms of tears, hysterical outbursts, jealousies, passionate, possessive love affairs with other women; a woman who complained about the interruptions from her readers, her friends, the daily domestic routine and said all she longed for was to be left alone to her art. But when she was, she was lonely and miserable and craved company, as she had always craved attention and affection. Her well was so empty, no one could ever fill it.

But I am enjoying this one of her journals all the same. She has an eye for beauty, an ability to describe a sky, a snow storm, a plant, a bird, a wild cat, the antics of her parrot Punch, so that one is there with her, and she was respectful of her country neighbours, whose lives were rough and poor and harsh but who had a dignity and a pride in manual work and an honesty which she valued.

Her best book is *The House by the Sea*, which will remain loved and understood when all the rest of her work has gone to oblivion. A salutary thought for any writer of any kind who takes themselves too seriously.

THE LAST DAY OF JANUARY, apropos of which a friend said, 'Now that can't be bad.' Yes and no. Yes, we are on the right side of the year – a little lighter in the mornings and evenings, more birds singing. And yet February and March and often April ('the cruellest month') can disappoint, and even May can be wet and windy and cold.

There is a way to go yet. The sedge is still withered from the lake.

———•○•———

YESTERDAY, I SAW a woman, bundled up in jackets and scarves and woolly hats, walking along the verge of a road picking up litter. She had a stick with a spike on the end of it and a black sack. But what a thankless task! No sooner has she gone along a stretch gathering stray papers and plastic pots and empty take-away containers than a few dozen thoughtless motorists speed by, windows open, the wind blows, and she has to start again. And then I remembered Ethel and a whole world clicked back into view.

Ethel was a friend of my aunt Doreen. They had been at university together – an unusual thing in itself for young women in the 1920s – and had both gone into teaching English. My aunt married – twice, as her first husband died very young. Ethel did not. When we lived in the Cotswolds, Doreen came to stay one summer and we were driving through a village a few miles from ours when she said, 'But this is where Ethel lives! I haven't seen her for thirty years.'

With the help of only her name (villages being helpful places), we quickly tracked Ethel down. She had retired from teaching English at Cheltenham Ladies' College many years earlier, and now she spent her time painting very good watercolours – and picking up litter. She went round the village and nearby lanes for two hours a day, with a black sack and a stick with a prong on the end.

After that, she and my aunt would spend a day together whenever Doreen came to stay, and after Doreen died and I was driving through Ethel's village, I saw her a few times and stopped to speak. Once, she invited me in for coffee. She was a very private, shy woman and I don't think she was altogether comfortable around people. But she did talk to me over that coffee about the Ladies' College in her day and particularly about the extremely good English department. I knew that the poet U. A. Fanthorpe had taught there and asked Ethel if she had known her. She looked awkward.

'She was a wonderful teacher. I liked her very much. I had the utmost respect for her. But then …'

Then?

She was silent for a moment, not looking at me. 'Then – she left. It was all very sad. A scandal, I'm afraid. They were both greatly missed. But of course they had no alternative.'

I had no idea, then, what she was talking about. I admired UA, as she was known, as a very fine poet indeed, but I knew little about her. So I looked a few things up, followed some links, and then, as soon as it came out, bought a copy of the book of poems she co-wrote with Rosie Bailey, *From Me to You.*

The poems are by them both, but they do not tell the reader which of them wrote which – although it's sometimes possible to guess, of course.

U. A. Fanthorpe and Rosie Bailey met at Cheltenham Ladies'

College, and worked alongside one another in the English department for seven years before, as they put it in the introduction to the book, 'We discovered that we liked one another.'

Liked was of course 'loved' and when they became partners, they left the school, Rosie to teach in a university, but UA, unexpectedly, to become a secretary/receptionist in a psychiatric hospital. It was then that she started to write poems in earnest. Rosie wrote them, too, though when she began is not clear. But it was UA who was the great poet.

They bought a house together, first in, of all places, Merthyr Tydfil, before moving to south Gloucestershire, where they were to live until UA's death in 2009. They seem to have been the perfectly matched married couple. The poems in this, their only joint collection, are a joy, and all of them good. They are tender, witty, warm, loving, revealing about everyday life – their cat, their dog, their home, their neighbours, the village, their public lives, their friends ... but most of all about each other.

I remember two things about them, in among all the rest. One is the poem 20.VIII.2003 about what birthday present the poet would, in a perfect world, give her partner – but cannot give because it includes items like 'the county of Devon, sea, valley, hill and moorland', and so the present is a bird feeder. The other is an observation about the party who sometimes walk the parish boundary.

There is always one,
Striding ahead with superior calves ...

I see that 'one' on the footpaths around here every day. It's the 'superior calves ...'

Look at their photographs. UA was a plump and homely looking woman who wore tweed suits and nice blouses with pussycat bows – absolutely what one of my English teachers wore, and generations of them before and, for a short time, after her. She sported very large, owl-like specs and a slightly bemused expression.

And Rosie Bailey. Look at her face alone and you see that it is soft and gentle. Kind. But she has cropped hair, wears a man's suit, leather belts, man's shoes, always – and I do mean 'man's'. One sees almost no women like this now, but the lesbian who could indeed, at first sight, be a man, who dressed and walked and talked like one, was a familiar figure from the 1920s on to the – what, 1970s? Especially among writers and artists. And why not? But it puzzles me that someone like U. A. Fanthorpe's partner felt that she had to look like a man. Maybe she didn't. Maybe that is just what she preferred.

U. A. Fanthorpe was a great poet, of that I have no doubt. The volume of her *New and Collected Poems* runs to 500 pages. She was interested in most things – the landscape of England and of the human heart. History. The way things seemed, as against the way they were. Christianity. The Church. Domestic life. Cats. Dogs. Birds. The garden. Whisky. Painters … The list is long.

I wish I had known her. I wish their partnership had not been, in its early days, some sort of scandal. Still, at least they lived happily ever after, until UA's death, and her literary star rides high in the firmament.

I get out the *New and Collected Poems*. 'For sixteen years … I'd been a teacher, dedicated to the cause of the un-split infinitive and the judicious use of the semi-colon,' she writes in her preface.

Carol Ann Duffy provides a short introduction which pinpoints two of UA's most important qualities:

> *This subtly subversive poet … understood the re-imagining of our traditions, the importance of the energy between the past and the present, particularly in poetry.*

And

> *[She] possessed an endearing patriotism that was founded lastingly on love, not shakily on superiority.*

Now there's a sentence to make one think. It could do to be written up in letters of gold somewhere, to teach those who deride patriotism and assume that it is always and everywhere A Bad Thing.

The collected poems are many. Surprising, looking through the fat volume, to see that UA only started writing them in 1974. She wasted too many years on the un-split infinitive.

Those by both her and Rosie Bailey, in *From Me to You*, are love poems and there is the crux of matter. As Ethel said, it was a quiet scandal though, Heaven knows, plenty of women schoolteachers lived together, in one capacity or another, without there being any raised eyebrows. There were certainly a couple of them at my grammar school. We giggled a bit and speculated on the colour of their satin bedspread, but I don't think anyone was shocked.

Once they had left Cheltenham Ladies' College, their lives fell into place with ease and they were rarely apart until UA's death. They were familiar figures on the poetry-reading circuit, much loved and apparently very accomplished in different ways, one complementing the other. I wish I had been to one of those evenings, though in general I hate having poetry read to me, especially 'with expression' – worst of all by actors but, almost as embarrassingly, by the poets themselves. Makes the toes curl.

How full of truth and love these love poems seem to be. They are gentle, committed poems. Nothing OTT about them, no jewelled imagery, no embarrassment of expression. I love them. Best-known, of course, is 'Atlas', which has become a cliché of the civil wedding …

> *There is a kind of love called maintenance.*
> *Which stores the WD40 and knows when to use it;*

But I think my favourite lines are:

> *I turn over pages, you say,*
> *Louder than any woman in Europe.*

U. A. Fanthorpe died of cancer. She and Rosie Bailey cemented their relationship of so many years with a civil partnership not long before she was taken ill. They both wore white – UA, a smart skirt suit; Rosie, as ever, a man's white trousers, shirt and jacket. They look comfortably settled and rather surprised, in the only photograph I have seen.

I wonder what Ethel would have thought. But I think Ethel must have died some time ago. For a year before I moved away from the Cotswolds, I had not seen her, walking the village bounds, picking up litter, a small, very bent figure, furious at the messy, thoughtless ways of more recent generations to whom no parent ever said, 'Now pick that up!'

———•◦•———

'PLEASE GIVE ME some idea of how you write?'

'I want to write a novel. Where do I begin?'

'I am doing an MA in Creative Writing. Please would you kindly tell me how many hours a day you write and how many drafts you do of a novel? I am finding that after about Draft 7 my work feels stale. Should that happen? Does it happen to you?'

'Would you consider running an online CW course? Or at least would you take on a few MA pupils and give them some guidance as to how exactly they should work, based on how you do it?'

And so on. They come in by email and via the website, but when I did a lot of lit fests and other book events the most-asked questions were also of this kind. People aspire to write – a very great many people – and they want help, to be told the tricks of the trade, given advice about how it is done/how they should do it. I think a lot of enquirers feel that if they knew how established/published writers work they would have the keys to the kingdom.

But there are no rules – there really are none. You do what you want, what feels right for you. I am the last writer to follow in this respect, any creative writing tutor would say so. I have let slip a few remarks about my way of working on the odd occasion when I have talked to MA students and not only are they surprised, even shocked, by what I have said – their tutors are horrified. Their method is to ask for draft after draft to be corrected, re-written, changed, after the previous ones have been read and 'corrected'.

How else would they spend/justify their time and salaries? All of this may work for some, but it would not work for me. I make some notes – sometimes a lot, more often just a few – and they are very random and disconnected. They are just my own aides-memoire. I think a lot. I probably do more thinking about a book than anything else, which is handy because you can do other things while you are thinking. And then I start. I carry on. I finish. One draft and one only, at least for fiction. Non-fiction usually requires a little re-arranging. Of course I tidy up and tighten up, I correct grammar and punctuation. But in all essentials, the first draft is the last draft is the published book. I can't work any other way. I never have. If I realise, a third or a half way into a book, that it is not working out, it doesn't 'feel' right or read right – and that has happened, if rarely – then I ditch the whole thing. After that, I have to wait a while before starting something new and quite different. Once or twice, I have gone back years later to the seminal idea for the one that didn't work, and picked it up again and it has fallen out easily. But mostly, if it is no good, it goes on being no good.

So do not be like me, I always say. Do not think this would work for you. It probably won't. I have had fifty-five years of experience but still every book is like walking a tightrope. I might fall off. But I could never do it with safety nets and harnesses. I couldn't write draft after draft.

I would never achieve an MA in Creative Writing.

FEBRUARY

MAKE A NOTE to myself. 'Buy more tulips.'

Even at this time of year, the local greengrocer, who sells the best cut flowers, has rows of zinc jugs out on the pavement, the tulips colour-coded – scarlet, ruby, orange, yellow, then coral, pink, blush, then purple, then white, cream, white with purple veining … green veining … They bring such vibrancy to an ordinary section of the high street. The shop people lay out their stalls as if this were a gallery – and so it is, of a delightful kind and cheaper than a lot of canvas art.

Purple cabbage. Red Cabbage. Cauliflower with purple not creamy white insides. Fresh green herbs. Juicy peas – imported for now, but still looking fresh-picked. Ditto asparagus. Tomatoes. Radishes. It is a joy to behold, this gallery, and they set it out every morning and dismantle and take it in every evening. I never understand people who say they can't afford fresh vegetables, because they are so cheap. You spend a fiver and come away with a big bagful. Fruit costs a bit more, but it's still cheaper than cake. I like both.

———•○•———

WHY DID I NOT LIKE fairy tales as a child? (By which I mean specifically stories that contain fairies, not stories which go under the same name but do not.) 'Sleeping Beauty', 'The Snow Queen', 'Cinderella', 'Hansel and Gretel', for example, appear in collections of 'fairy' stories but they do not refer to a single fairy. On the other hand, they are not folk tales either, so what do you call them? As a child I liked those twee little books of Flower Fairies by Cicely Mary Barker, with illustrations I pored over, but they are just an excuse for pretty pastel pictures. The Mountain Ash Fairy. The Lilac Fairy. The Buttercup Fairy. There was even a Groundsel Fairy.

I still don't like what I had better call 'stories about fairies.' I used to look at the row of Andrew Lang's Fairy Books of different colours, the Red, Blue, Yellow, Green, Violet, in the children's library and even if I were starved for something new to read, I never borrowed one. I took them down, opened them, flicked through to see if the stories had somehow become more acceptable to me, more exciting, more ... more anything really, except more of the same. But they never had. They were still fairies and I always closed the book.

I bought a beautiful copy of *The Violet Fairy Book*, a hardback, with gold and silver embossing on cloth, in a sturdy slipcase. It was £5 in a charity shop, still shrink-wrapped. I had to take it home because I somehow guessed that no one else would.

It is up there and yesterday I pulled off the shrink wrap and dived in. Fairies. Wispy, wafty, wishy-washy things. Nowhere near on a par with sprites and goblins, witches, wizards, trolls. As a child I lapped up stories about any of these. I can understand why I did not, and do not, have any patience with fairies and their stories. They are so colourless (despite Andrew Lang's best attempts). So dull. Yes. Just dull.

What does our individual taste in matters like this, matters that actually *don't* matter, say about us? I wish I could understand.

I am not keen on folk tales either. Or folk songs. Cecil Sharp must have been a bore.

———•◦•———

YESTERDAY, A NEIGHBOUR walking her dog in the opposite direction stopped to say she had just seen two HUGE herons in the water meadow. Never seen any so big.

Well, the male heron may be slightly larger than the female, as with many birds and other species, but not all that much. Still, I thought nothing more of it until this morning, when I saw the two HUGE herons by our own pond. So huge they could not be herons. They were cranes.

My bird-watching guru Samuel West, of acting fame, said he hadn't seen one for years – and Sam has seen everything. So I looked them up and found that there is a crane conservation and breeding programme going on at the bird reserve some six or seven miles from here. Which explains it. It is so often down to some local hero who takes charge of preserving or re-introducing a bird or other creature at risk. Cranes at Pensthorpe. Stone curlews on the van Cutsem estate, near Swaffham. Paul Getty's red kites at Wormsley Park in Buckinghamshire – which have virtually taken over the M40 corridor.

I have my own thoughts about allowing certain hawks special status, mind you. Buzzards and kestrels are as cheap as chips now and are responsible for killing thousands of song birds. This is what happens when we blunder in and start altering the balance of nature. But I have no idea what the answer is. As a friend said recently, 'For a start, you could shoot your cat.'

———•◦•———

I WISH IT WOULD SNOW. Snow is a magic substance. Snow muffles the world out there and locks you into its own, a strange form of peacefulness and stillness – except that when you walk through snow, it creaks.

Without looking them up, I can think of four books called simply *Snow*.

Without looking them up I remember others with snow in the title. *Miss Smilla's Feeling for Snow*. *Snow Falling on Cedars*. Both of those are books that, a couple of decades ago, absolutely everybody was reading. Is anybody reading them now? Then I will. I cannot remember anything about them.

And then there is perhaps the best of all classic children's stories, *The Snow Queen*, which C. S. Lewis peered into for his Narnia books, especially *The Lion, the Witch and the Wardrobe*.

A book I have treasured for half a lifetime is Johannes Kepler's *The Six-Cornered Snowflake*. Complex and complicated. Simple and clear. Snowflakes, like human fingerprints – no two are alike. But whereas fingerprints are intriguing, they are not mysteriously beautiful like snowflakes.

The cause of the six-sided shape of a snowflake is none other than that of the ordered shapes of plants and of numerical constants; and since in them nothing occurs without supreme reason – not, to be sure, such as discursive reasoning discovers, but such as existed from the first in the Creator's design and is preserved from that origin to this day in the wonderful nature of animal faculties, I do not believe that even in a snowflake this ordered pattern exists at random.

It was Kepler who said that all he was doing as a scientist and explorer of the natural and mathematical order of things was 'thinking God's thoughts, after Him'. But it is woeful to find that, in spite of his genius, his great scientific and linguistic mind, Johannes Kepler was not only an astronomer but the very last of all serious astronomers to be an astrologer, too. He believed that every child was moulded and influenced for the rest of its life by the configuration of stars and planets at the moment of its birth, as do a lot of people now. But I have yet to hear of any scientist who does.

I bet that is because there are none.

———•○•———

SO COLD. The blackbirds have started low-key singing every morning, and a male and a female have been chasing one another round a bush, but the bitter wind from Siberia will put paid to all that. The gangs of long-tailed tits are getting through fat balls at the rate of three a day.

———•○•———

FIVE BOOKS. There is a website someone told me about which has an archive of people who have chosen five books on a theme and been interviewed about their choices. At a decent length, too – so, not just a list. Jay McInerney has five novels of New York – including Edith Wharton's *The House of Mirth*, I am pleased to see.

Five Books on the History of Christianity (Diarmaid MacCulloch)
Five Books on London (Peter Ackroyd)
Five Books on Religious and Social History in the Ancient World (Robin Lane Fox)

On ...

The History of Reading
Eugenics
Divine Women
Aviation History
Revolutionary Russia
Social History of Post-war Britain (David Kynaston)
The Second World War (Anthony Beevor)
Christmas
British Prime Ministers
Royal Biographies
Oliver Cromwell
Chick Lit
Twentieth-century Theatre
Bestsellers (Jeffrey Archer)

It is hard to find a subject that has not been included, so let me try.

Fashion
The 1960s
Political Scandals
Biographies of Horses

A pleasant way to pass an idle half hour. Reading the archive of interviews on the website is absorbing and educative and gives you more ideas for your Must Read list than you could get through in a lifetime. You can only take in three or four at a time if you concentrate on studying the lists properly and include your own Agree or Disagree, Reasons to.

Some give you a whole new way of looking at a subject. I had been working steadily through the new Cambridge Latin series, enjoying it, remembering this, ashamed to have forgotten that, intending to get back up to A Level standard again, but then I read Harry Mount on Five Best Books about Learning Latin only to discover that the Cambridge is apparently despised as 'soft option teaching', no rigour, no need to learn the grammar before you can start reading authors. Harry Mount is for the old way of rote learning and I am for that, too, in terms of spellings and times tables, but if a new generation is going to be introduced to the joys and richness of Latin, especially a generation of young people not naturally inclined to the Classics, a new way had to be found and Cambridge has found it. Young people come to Shakespeare now via graphic novel versions of the plays. If they then go on to study the real thing and, even better, see them in the theatre, then that is surely good. Mount is a stickler for the steep and narrow way and of course that was how we all learned Latin and yes, it is the ideal way, the way of the purist. It just doesn't work for everyone now.

Perhaps the best test of what sort of a reader you are is to try compiling your own Five Best Books on … – and no looking up anything, anywhere, not even on a trip to your own shelves.

I tried it with Five Best Ghost Stories. Five Best Books by and about Edith Wharton, Thomas Hardy and Kitchen Sink writers. And books about Edward VIII and Wallis Simpson.

------■•○•■------

SNOWDROPS. ACONITES. No crocuses (croci?). Nothing much

else, so I spent a fortune on more cut tulips. Orange. Scarlet. Deep red. Plus some pink and white parrot tulips that were twice the price and half the quality. They just flopped over the edge of the vase. You don't always get what you pay for.

Not the weather for standing around more than two minutes admiring the spring flowers, the weather for clearing out book-shelves. If we ever leave this house, we will not want to start doing it as the removal men are at the door. I thought I had cleared out all the books I would ever need to lose five years ago, but books breed. They beget second copies because you have mislaid the first and buy another, the day before you find the first. They inter-breed, too, so you have *The Cambridge Companion to the Bible* next to the Oxford ditto, and several copies of Quentin Bell's biography of Virginia Woolf next to the one by Hermione Lee.

And whenever I go to the shelves to start an hour of de-stock-ing, I come upon a forgotten treasure. What I found today made me sad.

I have written previously about the last time I met Iris Murdoch, when dementia had taken a pretty strong hold on her but I had forgotten that, only weeks beforehand and not knowing anything about her state, I had sent her my copy of a recently compiled collection of her *Occasional Essays*, edited by Yozo Muroya and Paul Hullah, and published in Japan by the University Educa-tion Press in 1998 in an edition of 500 copies. It is a hardback, without a dustwrapper, but with a photograph on the front of one of Iris's paintings, of the Royal Oak pub in Steeple Aston, the village in Oxfordshire where she and John Bayley once lived. It has a delightful, unusual colour photograph of Iris on the back, Iris smiling rather mischievously, her badly cut hair (John used to do it with the kitchen scissors and they were probably blunt) raying out with the sun behind it.

I had sent the book to ask Iris if she would sign it, as I had often done with her books in the past. She always obliged and returned them, in previously much-used envelopes or jiffy bags, with several layers of other addresses and franked stamps already there. The book of essays did come back, though it took longer than usual, and the envelope was as pre-loved as ever. I did not know what to make of the inscription, though, and remained puzzled by it until I discovered about her illness.

Clearly, John has put the book in front of her, opened it at the title page and told her what to write. It looks as if it were done by a 3-year-old. It reads SUSAN in primitive wobbly capitals, then there is a vague wandering penline, and then IRIS.

She would not have had any idea what she was writing, or who I was – perhaps even who IRIS was. John must have read it out letter by letter.

Of course, I would never have sent it to her had I known. But I did not know. When I found out, I was horrified, but also did not quite know whether John had tried to be kind to me, and helpful to Iris, in keeping her going, pen to paper, or if he should not have done so but simply sent the book back unsigned, with a line of explanation. I have always felt that, in writing his memoir of her decline and then in allowing it to be filmed – the whole sad, sad detailed saga of it – he had betrayed her and, above all, betrayed her dignity. She had no say, no opportunity to say no – or, of course, to say yes.

I look at the handwriting now and I am sad beyond words – yet glad to remember her, too, even in this way, even as I see almost the very last handwriting of that great novelist, powerful thinker. Good friend.

———•○•———

THERE ARE ALWAYS SNOWDROPS for my birthday, and so there are today, a few green spears pushing up. I planted hundreds at the Cotswolds farmhouse over my twenty-five years there and they multiply by themselves as well, so hundreds became thousands. The best display I knew then was in the churchyard at Batsford, near Moreton-in-Marsh. It was worth driving out of one's way for, and then, if the day was unseasonably warm, sometimes also to see a new foal in the field, nuzzling up to its mother.

No foals here. Norfolk is the least horsey of all the counties I have ever known. I don't think there is even a hunt. It isn't much of a sheep place either, though there are a few small flocks round here. No horses. No sheep. Instead, pigs. Pigs and sugar beet. And churches. And the sea. The sea.

———•○•———

I DRIVE OVER TO CLEY and struggle up the shingle bank, one step forward two back, as the heaps of stones shift and slide and re-shape themselves beneath my feet. The sea is roaring. Not even the boldest, hardiest of swimmers today, and no fishermen, no families. Two other people, walking their dogs. I haven't brought Poppy. Shingle is very unkind to a dog's feet. I stand and watch the breakers folding over and over and crashing down, sending up creamy spray like massive fireworks bursting open in the sky. Then collapsing before raking and rasping back over the shingle again. As Tennyson said:

Break, break, break
On thy cold grey stones, O sea.

If you have been born and bred by the sea, you can be content watching it for hours. I sit for a while – Walter Benjamin says somewhere that the natural prayer of the soul is attentiveness – but the wind comes off the water, north-easterly, flaying my skin.

I found a great quote for a birthday, too, from May Sarton's *Journal of Solitude*: 'Do not deprive me of my age. I have earned it.' It gives the lie to all those who want to remain young, and although they surely must know that they cannot do that, they still give it a go, via facelifts and Polyfilla.

———•○•———

INSOMNIA. VERY UNTYPICAL. In the end I start listing all the novels I have read – and when I get desperate, those I mean to read, and, more desperate still, have ever heard of, going through the alphabet. I have no laptop or other e-device in the bedroom, so I cannot cheat via Google and it is far too cold to get out of bed and consult bookshelves. Rule is, as many titles as you like for each letter, but you have to move on after twenty seconds.

A is for … *Animal Farm* … *All Quiet on the Western Front* … *Alice in* …

It is interesting how few new novels leap to my mind whenever I play this game. Everything on my list is either an old favourite or a school or university set text. I suppose that's because they have been in my memory for so long that they have become embedded, like fossils, and new books are still proving themselves. I should try listing only books published in the last couple of years and see how far I get – not very, is my guess. Or do it with non-fiction. Or children's books. There would be far fewer titles under each letter, and I would probably fall asleep around G. Which is, after all, the point of the exercise.

————•○•————

FLIPPING THROUGH a couple of books about books, in search of an elusive title I don't find, I find instead that I can make a pretty decent list of 'Authors I Have Never Read.'

Sartre. Kafka. Wyndham Lewis. Knausgaard. Italo Svevo. Zane Grey. Orhan Pamuk. Terry Pratchett. Philip K. Dick. Georges Duhamel … and on and on. Interesting how almost all are non-English writers. Of course I have not read every great English novelist or poet, but when I look at a standard chronology I do seem to have covered an awful lot of ground. Of course I have. I read English at a time when one still began with the Anglo-Saxons and moved on down the centuries through Chaucer and *Piers Plowman* to Shakespeare, the Metaphysical poets and Donne, and so to Dryden and Pope and then, at last, the novel – Richardson, Fielding, *Tristram Shandy*, the ludicrous Gothic novel … and, the mighty Victorians. English Literature stopped officially at 1880. Then Modern Literature began and that, like American Literature and philology, one could take as a special option, which of course I did.

But I am under-read in whole areas that matter. Or at least I have always understood, aka been told, that they matter. I ought to discover the truth for myself but Kafka never seems to beckon very seductively.

————•○•————

... which hath twenty-eight days clear,
And twenty-nine in each Leap Year.

THE JINGLE WE ALL KNEW and on which I still rely. I must try and pass these on to my grand-daughter. She has been introduced to nursery rhymes and many folk and fairy stories, if only via Disney – and better Disney than not at all.

Time for 'Thirty days hath September ...'

————•○•————

BLOOD-CURDLING LINES. Number 1.

'Footprints?'

'Footprints.'

'A man's or a woman's?'

Dr Mortimer looked strangely at us for an instant, and his voice sank almost to a whisper as he answered:

'Mr Holmes, they were the footprints of a gigantic hound!'

The Hound of the Baskervilles is the best of all Sir Arthur Conan Doyle's Sherlock Holmes stories. Other people might pick other stories, and it is surprising, given their lasting and worldwide popularity, how few of these there actually are, though Conan Doyle wrote plenty of other things.

Sherlock Holmes has become not just a Victorian detective in a series of short novels and stories, he has become one of those iconic literary figures who take on a life of their own, out of the context of their books. Is 221b Baker Street the best-known fictional address? People visit Haworth Parsonage, Beatrix Potter's cottage in the Lake District, Dickens's London house … but how many who visit the commercial museum at 221b Baker Street realise that it is a fabrication?

The nearest book to Conan Doyle's stories that I can think of which has entered the general public consciousness and has enjoyed as many re-creations in other media by other writers – films, stage plays, television series, new versions simplified for children, and so on – is Dickens's A *Christmas Carol*. Scrooge has become a synonym for miser. Even today, millions know who Tiny Tim was. This best known and loved of all Christmas stories, other than the original one in the Bible, this rival to every other ghost story has been re-invented scores of times. And the original novel still comes up as fresh as a daisy.

I wonder if recent TV attempts to tell new Holmes stories, to put him in times, places and situations that would have been alien to him, have brought more sales for the books themselves? I hope so. Because Conan Doyle invented one of the greatest literary characters of all time. The setting, the times, the atmosphere, the detail, but above all the man himself, grab the reader and hold the reader, for life. Close your eyes and picture Holmes's rooms. You can. See him, his own eyes closed, pipe in mouth, lost to everything around him, while he works out a complicated case which has been brought to him. Hear him play his melancholy violin. Observe him as he leaves the house to get into a hackney cab, deerstalker on head, whistling for the Baker Street irregulars (another version of Fagin's boys in *Oliver Twist*). Then see him with magnifying glass in hand, examining a footprint in the soil of a flowerbed beneath a window. See him striding across Dartmoor. See him in disguise, as an old beggar, a cab driver, muffled to the eyes in big coat and scarf … And we can. We do. We could step into his world and be fully familiar with it in a heartbeat. We do not need any film to show us what it looks like.

Holmes preceded many a detective who outstrips PC Plod at every turn, who has a sidekick, who is a loner with a mysterious past, and who has flaws in his character and behaviour. Indeed, most fictional detectives since, private or police, owe a lot to him. It has become part of the template to give them idiosyncrasies, oddities, something that sets them apart from the normal run of men (and they were virtually all men, for a century or more). This, of course, makes for interesting reading and puts them in a class above the average copper, which is as it should be. One can fully understand why the latter got fed up with Sherlock Holmes and his successors, demonstrating their superior brains and powers of deduction.

It is atmosphere as well as the quirkiness of the hero that sets Conan Doyle's fiction above the rest, and in *The Hound of the Baskervilles* he excels himself – though what writer could fail, setting his scene on deserted, misty Dartmoor, to which the tree-lined avenue of a lonely house leads?

I have always felt that, although the terrifying, gigantic, baying hound, with its phosphorescent eyes and panting, foggy breath, is a magnificent creation, the murderers, before and after being unmasked, are rather underwhelming, and of course the solution is a cheat. Phosphorous would have half-blinded the dog the second it touched its eyes, and in any case, would never have given off more than a faint gleam. Still, we suspend disbelief and indeed, although once we know explanation and solution we can never unknow them, the story holds up after many a re-reading – which is not the least of its author's achievements.

A book that cannot be returned to again and again, and still yield fresh entertainment and insights, is only half a book.

De-stocking again. Out go the ephemeral detective stories you will never re-read, and duplicate copies, the books that don't belong to me, the books that have had coffee or wine spilled over them, been left out in the rain or fallen into the bath and retrieved, more in hope than in expectation of a good outcome.

The most difficult decisions are to do with the small collections I have made. Most people have obsessions and these usually come and go. Once you have fallen out of love with your passion, you do not want books about it to take up several yards of shelf space, though you may feel fond and nostalgic enough to save one. Or perhaps two.

Here are four whole long shelves of books by and about Virginia Woolf and the Bloomsbury Set. Now this is difficult. Of course I will keep copies of VW's novels, her *A Writer's Diary* and a couple of biographies – probably the short, succinct one by Quentin Bell, which contains nearly all you need to know, and the long one by Hermione Lee, which brings things up to date – well, up to a decade ago anyway. I doubt if much that is new, except a pencilled shopping list, is likely to come to light now, though occasionally there are surprises in the 'about' category. But the Woolf ocean has been pretty well trawled.

Do I keep the complete sets of her letters and diaries? Do I keep the books about VW and someone else – Vita Sackville-West, Lytton Strachey? Do I keep Leonard's own books?

And then there's the lit crit. Some of it is very good. Informative. Illuminating. Much is transient – the fashionable gender and

LGBT and childhood abuse stuff can go. The Cambridge Companions always stay. But recollections of VW's great aunts and her housekeepers?

What about the principal figures of 'Bloomsbury' – the books about Vanessa Bell and Duncan Grant, their art and their houses?

The essays by or about other Bloomsbury-ites – John Maynard Keynes, Lytton Strachey again, Dora Carrington, Roger Fry? Even Dame Ethel Smyth?

Oh help.

My Marilyn Monroe obsession is more easily dealt with because these are mainly books of photographs, the same or similar ones endlessly repeated. I pick out the best and most representative. I wonder if almost as many people have jumped on the MM bandwagon as on the Virginia Woolf one.

There really is nothing new on the biography front. I will keep Sarah Churchwell's very good book about Marilyn but ditch the rest. That reduces about forty books down to four in no time.

Wood engravings. I used to have a passion for them. I still love them. But not three shelves' worth of love.

Medieval monasticism, with a sub-heading, 'Cistercians in the Eleventh Century'. Big books. Small books. Academic books. Topographical. Illuminated.

Elizabeth Bowen, all her work and four biographies, plus too much lit crit.

Benjamin Britten and Aldeburgh. Suffolk and the Festival. Shelf after shelf. I doubt if they will be of interest to anyone now. The centenary was the time to dispose of the best. My Britten obsession is long over.

And so it goes on …

People say they can never part with a book. I can. As fast as I get one out of the back door, two new ones come in through the front anyway.

—•O•—

ANY DAY NOW I will look up from my desk and see the woman from up the lane, with her fishing net, peering down our drains. Normal for Norfolk.

The frogs are on the move from wherever they have been for months – under stones, in muddy holes (I don't know, one never sees them) – along the lane, through the grass and the ditches, making their way to our pond for the mating season. Soon there will be frogspawn, that joy of small children's nature outings, and then tadpoles in jars on the classroom window ledge. But on their mysterious journeyings, some frogs find their way into our drains and that would be that, were it not for the eccentric neighbour. She comes pottering along and is to be seen lifting grids and manhole covers and, from time to time, plunging her fishing net into them, occasionally to pull it out full of frogs. Well, possibly not 'full', but containing the odd one. These she transports lovingly and safely across to the pond and plunges the net in, to release the dear little amphibians. It is a mission of mercy and of conservation, though I wouldn't bother, the world having as many frogs and toads as it can handle. But there is no arguing with the neighbour, so we let her probe into our drains to her heart's content.

MARCH

CAME IN LIKE A LION. The first early tulips in our garden are flayed by the wind.

Driving from Salthouse, I was almost hit by a heron lofting up from the marsh to my left, long umbrella legs dangling. Pterodactyl.

Am reading *The New Book of Snobs* by the versatile D. J. Taylor. It is fairly spot on but makes one or two incorrect assumptions about the aristocracy. The thing about snobbery, surely, is that it is harmless if it means that people look up to others, never when it means that they look down. Andrew, 11th Duke of Devonshire, was the least snobbish man one could meet, and cared greatly for the estate people and those who came to visit Chatsworth and the Park. He never patronised. But he knew his place and his ducal role all right. I daresay he looked up, in the traditional, hierarchical way, to royalty, as forming the only social layer above his own. Some dukes have been – probably still are – absolute shits. But then, so are plenty of other people. It is not a question of their having the money and the land and the houses, it's what they do with them. Andrew gave away a lot of money, and he also shared widely what he regarded as his only 'on loan'.

Which brings me to his wife Debo. D. J. Taylor called her 'the most terrifying woman I have ever met'. She could be, though I didn't find her so – but then, very few people terrify me in that way. I am not awed by rank as rank.

A friend says that Debo was as hard as nails. Nearly twenty years ago, I enjoyed thinking up, editing (with Sophy Topley, her younger daughter) and publishing Debo's book, *Counting My Chickens* … We had massive amounts of fun. Faxes were all the rage in 2002 and Debo never stopped asking questions by fax, demanding daily sales figures and telling jokes. It brightened up the late afternoons considerably. My small publishing company sold many thousands of that book, and it rode high on the best-seller lists for ages. Her dedication reads 'To the co-editors, with love'. So I must have done something right.

But one day, about a year after it was published, I received a tiny envelope in the post which contained a letter on a tiny sheet of paper. I am not exaggerating. She was given to using very small sheets of headed notepaper inside very small envelopes. In this letter, Debo told me that she had put together a second volume of her pieces – my heart leaped – and that it was to be called *Home to Roost*. John Murray was to publish it. It was a done deal.

What I did wrong and why she did not think my small publishing house worthy of her any more, I will never know, because we never communicated again. I was deeply hurt and very upset. We had been friends, as I thought, as well as working colleagues. I loved her and I admired her enormously. I put together and had privately printed a book of lovely 'tributes' – wrong word – *To Debo, on Her 85th Birthday. From Her Friends*. So many funny, warm, witty, delightful letters to and about her came in after I requested people to write something about her, and the Prince of Wales wrote a loving foreword. It made her cry when she got her copy.

I loved Debo. I admired her.

So, one never knows. Hey ho.

————◆•○•◆————

FUNNY OLD COUNTY, Norfolk, though as I have only lived here for five years I suppose that I am not entitled to comment. And I will never feel 'Norfolk' any more than I felt 'Gloucestershire'. What does this mean? It is a sort of patriotism, of the right kind. It is an instinctive rooted-ness in the corner of the country where one first saw the light of day. It is attachment. Love. Yes. But an adopted county can never be the same. I have lived in other counties for far longer than I lived in Yorkshire, where I was born, but they haven't left much trace.

Will Norfolk? No. There is a lot of county snobbery here. The 'royal county'. Lots of deference. Then there is the red-trousered brigade, in August and on fine weekends. There is also a small corner of those aristo-hippies, living in some of the nicest old houses. Posh names and no money. They are Lefties, too, which I think must be a hangover from their Flower Power youth. Otherwise, there are still plenty of Norfolk born-and-bred builders and flint masons and tractor and sugar beet men. You still hear the accent round here. I wish I could do it but I'll never 'get' Norfolk, any more than I can get Liverpool. I can even do Northern Ireland before those. And Edinburgh Morningside.

————◆•○•◆————

WE ARE OUT ON A LIMB here, of course. Too far from the train. Too far for anyone to pop over for a night. Bad roads. Awful road accidents. No motorways. It is not as flat as Noel Coward said – there are hills round this house and within the nearby five square miles. But not hills as in Yorkshire and the Cotswolds. Not serious hills.

I love the skies. The sea. The fact that it is locked off. But if I ever go from Norfolk, I won't have left any of my heart behind.

Meanwhile, friends have gone to live in Theresa May's village in Berkshire.

Talking of which, the usual crop of political memoirs bow the legs of the bookshop tables around now. Why do they all think they must write so much? Oh, the money – yes, of course. But if they cut their books down to a manageable size they might sell more copies. And people might read them.

———•○•———

SPRING IS NOT GREEN at all, it's yellow. Aconites. Crocuses. Daffodils. Gorse. Primroses. Forsythia. Buttercups and dandelions. This year, because the winter has been so mild, the trees are already just brushed with the first leaves. In some lights they look pale pink, in others orange. Then lemony lime.

Last night, I thought there was a tawny owl in the sitting room, its twoo-whit twoo-whoo was so loud and clear and near. Then I realised that it was sitting on the chimney pot and its voice was echoing down into the wood burner, which was out but whose doors were open. Extraordinary sound. I went to look out into the night and heard another, somewhere beyond, answering. Two wagtails were chasing one another over the book store roof, and a female blackbird was scurrying away from a male, but not really, under the hedge.

———•○•———

I ANSWER A LETTER from an aspiring novelist – not one of those who just wants to make 'as much money as J. K. Rowling' (which was in a recent message) but who actually wants to write for writing's sake. To tell stories. To see her name on a book jacket. I am sure that making a living from her writing has indeed entered her thoughts and I could copy out one of those surveys which show what the miserable annual income of 90 per cent of novelists is. But why be a killjoy at this stage? She will find out soon enough.

I was lucky to be mentored and befriended at an early age and stage by the novelist and critic Pamela Hansford Johnson and her husband C. P. Snow. And maybe here I go again, lamenting that 'nobody reads their books now'. That is almost certainly true. Snow's novels have dated badly. The eleven-volume *Strangers and Brothers* sequence, autobiographical, of course – Snow was a recorder, not a man of imagination – trace the life of a young man, Lewis Eliot, from a poor background in Leicester – where Snow himself was born – to the Corridors of Power. So many things have changed in public life and in the sort of career path such a man could have, beginning in the 1920s, that it is inevitable that the series seems somewhat fusty. But there is one outstanding book in the sequence which can be read and re-read today with as much involvement and excitement as when it was first published. That is *The Masters*.

Any novel has a headstart when the core plot focuses on an election – rather like the contents of a will or the discovery of a body. In this case, the Master of a Cambridge college – not named but modelled on Snow's own old college, Christ's – is dying. He has been an exemplary Master and a good man, he has cancer, and his doctors have advised that he should not be told that his illness is terminal, so that he can enjoy his last months in peace and optimism. That, of course, would not happen now, but it was common medical advice up to thirty years ago or so. Naturally, a new Master must be chosen and so factions start to form within the college. There are two stand-out candidates, unless the college 'looks outside' – and in those days again, such a thing almost never happened. (Now it is the norm at both Oxford and Cambridge.)

The candidates are Paul Jago, a warm, sympathetic, genuine man who wears his heart on his sleeve, who is liked, even loved, and who would make a good Master in the mould of the current one. He has two major flaws. He is volatile and emotional – not a steady pair of hands. And he has an appalling wife – an uppity, rude, self-absorbed, pompous, snobbish woman. Only he can see her good qualities, such as they are, and then only because he looks with the eyes of love. But in truth Jago knows everything about his wife's character only too well.

The second candidate is Thomas Crawford, an eminent scientist, important member of the Royal Society, efficient, self-confident and entirely self-blind. He is cold and has few friends and cares not a jot about it. He will make the best Master in many ways, but he has few redeeming qualities and no human warmth.

The college duly divides and the Jago faction seem to have a clear majority, and to go on having it – until one or two unexpected events occur. Minds and sides are changed, and the result is no longer a foregone conclusion.

As a novelist, Charles Snow was more interested in character than plot, but in *The Masters* he engages our passion to know who voted for whom and what the outcome was, as well as the fascinating machinations and plottings of a caucus which is sure it can, and will, get its candidate in. He found the ambitions of men in their spheres of work – academia and politics and world affairs, most of all – of endless interest and he analyses them in each of the novels in the sequence. Business was of lesser importance, but the dynastic sense counted for quite a lot. He also looks into love and marriage but in this area he does not always convince, though he understood hopeless passion very well.

Charles Snow was very like his books. He was generous and kind to me, as a young writer, and those things count, in the end, far more than some quirks of character and behaviour. What survives of his desire to be important in the world, and his ambition to be influential in it, may be precious little, but his novels deserve to be read – and not only as accurate surveys of British life in the twentieth century but as sympathetic and compassionate studies of humanity.

——•○•——

IF I HAD BEEN ASKED who invented writing, I would have replied correctly: the Babylonians. I don't know how I know this but I do. Yet if I think back to how long ago cave men drew pictures on cave walls, I presume writing must have come later. But maybe not much later, in overall terms. I presume wrong. The Babylonians invented writing only 5400 years ago. That sounds a very long time ago but, after all, Jesus lived 2000 years ago. After writing came alphabets came words came languages came scribes came scrolls came reading ...

I have not yet discovered when man discovered numbers, and so mathematics. Or did man 'discover' numbers? Did man discover words? Or were they there all the time, like the stars and the planets, waiting to be discovered?

I pick up a book and look at it and then remember how even more recently it was that man invented printing. Pretty much yesterday.

My head buzzes.

———•○•———

TOOK SOME BOOKS to the charity shop. Included a couple of my own, spare paperbacks.

Nice lady serving. 'Oh, thank you so much. Oh, and a Susan Hill book! She is very popular.'

SH: I'm pleased to hear it.

NLS: Actually – here are two on the shelf that are *signed* copies.

SH: Wow!

NLS: Oh yes. (Leans over confidentially.) We can get 10p more for them if they are signed.

———•○•———

THE GEESE WENT OVER in one of their magnificent skeins, reminding me that they will be off back to Siberia before long and then we will have to wait a few weeks for the hirundines. It is a strange thing. The skies are full of huge, ungainly, slow-moving geese. I watch them descend, swirling round, lower and lower, until they touch down on the marshes one day, and then the same skies are empty, blank and vast and grey or blue. But anticipation builds again. The first swallow appears, usually on a telegraph wire, the advance party before days, even sometimes a week or two, later, and then another anxious wait for the rest, and then for the house martins to dip towards their old nests in the eaves, vanish, return, swoop fast into them and so start the old dance. The swifts come last and leave first, and so are the most precious. They never land. The only time they are settled and with firm ground, as it were, beneath their feet, is when they are born and brought up in their nest. The second they are fledged, they are airborne for pretty well the rest of their lives. They should be here by the first week in May, but sometimes it is later, and then it is a worry that they will not have time to rear a brood. Somehow they always do, and often two. But by the first week in August, they, too, those acrobats of the skies, will be gone thousands of miles just as the geese are thinking of returning across thousands more, from a different direction.

How astonishing it all is. And somehow, very wasteful of energy and time. Yet if they were here all the year round, would we like that? Would there be room? We certainly would not value them so much.

———•◦•———

THESE LAST FEW DAYS have been occupied by actors not birds, as I took a trip to London for various meetings, and a visit to the theatre to see *An Inspector Calls*. Is this the only work by J. B. Priestley that not only has survived, but will go on surviving? *When We are Married* is an excellent play and I wish someone would revive that in a modern form as striking and fresh as *An Inspector*. Why don't they?

Nothing else of his holds up. No one reads his novels now, or his essays or his stories. Although *Time and the Conways* is put on from time to time.

He would not have been philosophical about this. JB cared dreadfully, painfully, about how his work was perceived and received, just as he cared desperately about his status and how he was seen by the world beyond his study. He longed to be awarded the Order of Merit – the highest honour of all that the Queen can bestow – and eventually, rather too late, he was.

He played the bluff, gruff Yorkshireman – and once he was, but he had moved far away from Bradford in every sense. He liked spacious living, a bit of grandeur, the wine and cigars and staff that money could buy. He could be self-important but he had a good heart, and he was generous with his hospitality.

He and his third wife Jacquetta were an unlikely pair. They had caused a certain amount of scandal by leaving their marriages for each other – scandal which would barely register now. By the time I met them, they were a settled, conventional – and devoted – married couple.

Evenings at their house – Kissing Tree House, named that by Jack because he said 'kissing is a lovely thing' – just outside Stratford-upon-Avon, were formidable. I found them nerve-wracking. The house was very formal, as were the evenings, and the ritual of them never varied. Greeted at the top of an imposing flight of steps by both JB and Jacquetta (in black tie and long dress respectively), one then walked down a marble corridor with niches on either side full of sculpture – busts and archaeological finds, all well lit and displayed. It was like walking down the corridor of a classical gallery. Drinks were served, the old-style drinks – gin, whisky, rum, sherry, dry martini, whatever you wanted – mixed by Jack. And champagne, always. The dining table was round, there was a careful placement, one was served by a butler, and the cooking, by their cook/housekeeper, was extremely good, plain English food. Conversation was led by Jack, and he was a good host, skilled at introducing his guests to one another.

The second time we went, I was heavily pregnant with my first daughter. I had been initially placed on Jack's right, an honour indeed, but when he saw me, he effected a swift table re-arrangement. 'I like you,' he said, quite seriously, 'but in your state, I'm frightened of you. I don't want you having a baby while you're sitting next to me.' So I was duly moved.

My daughter was born a week later and the NHS maternity home was across a meadow from the Priestleys' house. When she heard the news, Jacquetta walked over one afternoon visiting hour. I was startled. She was very charming but somehow did not at all fit into the surroundings of a ward of sixteen new mothers. My baby was in her cot at the side of my bed and every other cot had gooing grandmothers and aunts and friends, waxing lyrical about the child's heavenly beauty. Jacquetta looked intently at my daughter for some ten seconds. Then she nodded.

'Nice and neat and compact,' she said, 'and that's all one can say at this stage.'

I did not feel cheated at the absence of fawning and gooing. I got plenty of that from everyone else. But Jacquetta was just not that sort of woman. I appreciated her visit very much.

I found her, as did many people, formidable, handsome rather than beautiful, very stately, wonderfully well dressed. Her evening gowns were couture. She was immensely intelligent, learned indeed, and she did not suffer fools. But she was kind to me. Jack died a short time after our second daughter was born prematurely, living for five weeks, and we went to his funeral, in Stratford's Guild Chapel. Jacquetta looked statuesque, contained, poised – and hauntingly grief-stricken.

A little time afterwards, she wrote to me about our dead daughter, apologising for not having done so at once – she had been fully occupied by Jack's illness and dying. Her letter was one of great compassion, understanding and tenderness and I will never forget it. Her guard was finally down and always after that, when we met, I felt differently about and towards her.

I liked Jack but I could never entirely get a handle on him. Maybe he was much simpler than one supposed and there were no great hidden depths. Maybe what you saw was what you got. He thought a lot of his own work, though he was modest about it in public. His novels do not hold up now. They are dated without being classic. The two plays will be revived from time to time. But I think he would have minded very much that no one much under the age of fifty has read or even heard of him – at least not beyond the brilliant revival of *An Inspector Calls* which is also a standard GCSE text these days. At least he would have been pleased about that.

------●•O•●------

WILD AND WUTHERING. There are several trees down in the fields around and also in the Bayfield woods. All old trees. You can see how rotten they are inside, just waiting for a strong wind. Looking around, I see so many more which are only just upright. They will be the next. Are we re-planting trees to replace them? I often look at London or other city streets – Oxford and Norwich are good examples – lined with wonderful mature trees and wonder about that, because the Victorians planted these and they are almost past their sell-by dates. Councils are forever closing roads to take down dangerous trees, but when they are all gone, how altered will our urban street landscapes be. Trees are green lungs for cities and shelter for birds and insect life. And beautiful. How many children never go near the country, but walk to school past trees that are bare, then in bud, in leaf, thick and heavily green through the summer holidays, but, as the new school year starts, begin to turn and then fall conkers. Ash keys. These trees could be their introduction to the natural cycle, but if we don't plant more – and I see no evidence that we are doing so – the streets will be bleak. The same goes for municipal parks, for which we owe the Victorians, again, such gratitude. But that fine thing, the National Lottery, has stepped in here and parks have been rescued from near-wildernesses to become again places where children play, the old sit on benches, mothers with babies chat and ducks swim on ponds and are fed.

Meanwhile, yesterday I saw a nuthatch in one of our spinney trees, then, after a moment, a tree creeper. The insect life in trees, which sustains these tiny birds, is unseen, unheard, and vital. Every time I read someone mentioning that we must save pandas and wolves and polar bears, I want to write letters to the paper about insects.

--------●•O•●--------

IN THE END I decided it was too dangerous to go out. Slates were flying. So I went up into the attic to open some mysteriously sealed boxes. I thought that I had found and shelved all the old Ladybird books … but there was another case. I sat on the floor and was lost in them until it grew dark. There are another two bookcases full in the children's bedroom, and grand-daughter Lila is now old enough to pick some out herself and take them off into a cosy corner. As I write this, she is only just beginning to read but the joy of the older Ladybirds – before around 1970 – has always been the pictures. I found her absorbed in a pile that included *Garden*

Birds, and *What to Look for in Winter*, and the one on her lap, which she was looking at intently, *Julius Caesar and Roman Britain*. I think I learned more from Ladybirds than I did from lessons. History. Heroes. Saints. Legends. Science. Nature. Great Artists. 'How It Works'. 'People Who Help Us'. Hobbies. I had also had them read to me, and in turn read myself, one or two of the early story rhymes. I still have them by heart.

From her little cottage window,
Mrs Downy Duck looked out:
Said, 'Oh, what a frosty morning!
What a lot of ice about!'

(I didn't look that up.)

The illustrations to the fairy stories, before someone had the bright idea of updating them, were doors into a particular world. *Cinderella. The Princess and the Pea. Beauty and the Beast.* I close my eyes and see the ball gowns of the Ugly Sisters and the satin breeches worn by Prince Charming ... The high high bed with its many mattresses and a single pea tucked under the bottom one ... The Old Queen answering the palace doorbell herself in the middle of the night ...

Several were such favourites I read them aloud over and over again, at innumerable bed times, yawning the while. *The Little Red Hen. Chicken Licken. The Enormous Turnip. The Magic Stone. The Magic Porridge Pot. The Gingerbread Man.* (When he was one quarter gone, being eaten by the fox, a small hand would shoot out and close the book so as not to hear or look, for What Happened Next was unbearable.)

Chicken Licken was the most boring. *The Enormous Turnip* not far behind.

If you want to be reminded about King Canute and the waves, or King Alfred and the burnt cakes, or Sir Walter Raleigh laying down his cloak over the puddle for Queen Elizabeth, there are Ladybird books for you to learn the essential stories in five minutes. What kind of nests wrens or jackdaws make, what Blackthorn or May blossom look like – all here with pretty clear pictures.

Some of the old Ladybirds have become wonderfully dated. Do not go to *The Computer* for any new electronic information, and fire engines and police cars look totally different today. Uniforms have all changed. How long since nurses wore swan-like white caps?

In later years, Ladybird tried to bring themselves up to date by grabbing trendy cartoon characters as they flashed by – Scooby-Do, Transformers, Superman. The pictures were ugly, and no sooner were the books out than the kids were way in the distance with something else.

And now variations on Ladybird books have sprung to life, and are given to adults as Christmas joke books, to put in the downstairs loo. They are read on Boxing Day and then are left behind wherever they fell ... *How It Works: The Dad. The Ladybird Book of the Hipster. The Ladybird Book of the People Next Door.* They are briefly funny, although maybe the best thing about them is the idea and then you can make up your own. I thought of doing a *Ladybird Book of the Hip Replacement*.

It is a cynical money-making ploy and it has worked. I am happy with publishers making money, cynically or not. They can always spend it on the rest of us. Meanwhile, I am back with *Ladybird Bible*

Stories: Moses Prince and Shepherd. If I pull one out at random, I never fail to find something that delights, teaches, reminds, makes me smile. And of how many book series can you say that?

———•○•———

THE EGRET, which has been around for a while now, has acquired a mate and there are signs of nesting. To think, these birds were almost extinct a hundred years ago. They still look primeval, though …. avian pterodactyls, like herons. There is something about herons that makes me shudder and I think the only reason I don't shudder at egrets, which are so like them in shape, is because egrets are white, like doves and angels.

———•○•———

TALKING OF EVIL, did anyone ever create a character as evil as Mr Hyde? Shakespeare, of course, in Iago, but he is altogether real and human, there is no touch of the chemistry lab about him. Some would say Dracula. But Dracula goes one step further, into pure fantasy and so is less frightening – to me, anyway. Not sure why, but I can just believe Dr Jekyll could turn into Mr Hyde. Vampires are the stuff of the legendary and the fantastic.

Robert Louis Stevenson's novella improves every time I read it. I generally find something new, something better, in its pages. Last night, I was struck by how cleverly and carefully and cunningly Stevenson creates a sense of both the sinister, which is mainly suggested by way of atmosphere and small detail, and the pure evil, which is seen, heard, experienced. Even though the narration begins calmly and the tone is measured, the screw has begun to turn in the very descriptions of the area of London in which Dr Henry Jekyll lives.

I was coming home from some place at the end of the world, about three o'clock of a black winter morning, and my way lay through a part of town where there was literally nothing to be seen but lamps. Street after street and all the folks asleep – street after street, all lighted up as if for a procession and all as empty as a church – till at last I got into that state of mind when a man listens and listens and begins to long for the sight of a policeman.

A few pages later, there is a scene set at nine o'clock in the morning, but when the first fog of the season has already begun to close in. The wind makes the clouds shift about so that one moment it seemed like dreadful night, the next, like a terrible brownish twilight. 'The dismal quarter of Soho seen under these changing glimpses, with its muddy ways and slatternly passengers … seemed, in the lawyer's eyes, like a district of some city in a nightmare.'

But it is the descriptions of Hyde which chill the reader to the bone. There are hints and suggestions … but in the end we are not given a clear, and full, detailed description of the man. We build it up ourselves from the author's half-glances.

Every time I read Stevenson's novella I am brought up short by how good it is. There is not a word out of place, he does not put a narrative foot wrong. The style, the structure, the quality of the writing, the creation of evil, and fear, and an atmosphere of pent-up near-hysteria … all of these make me admiring and envious. Next to Dickens, I think RLS was the greatest writer of his time.

———■•O•■———

I AM NOT GOING OUT again probably until June. The wind is like a razor blade shaving off a layer of skin.

———•○•———

I WAS THINKING that when we read as children we just give ourselves over to the book. The story. The characters. The places. The atmosphere. We immerse ourselves in it, we soak ourselves. On the whole, we are uncritical, too, or at least critical only in a very simple way. 'I loved that.' 'I want to read the next one like that.' Or 'I didn't like that story.' 'It was a bit boring.' Nothing more sophisticated, no reasons given, none necessary. I remember trying to read *Swallows and Amazons* and getting perhaps one third of the way before abandoning it, and then doing the same again, and then trying one or two others of Arthur Ransome's stories and doing the same. I could not relate to the children, I had no idea what sailing was all about – sailing for me was on the sea, trawlers out catching fish, or me standing watching the odd pleasure steamer round Scarborough Bay, a lifeboat being launched. But these children who lived in a place, the Lake District, that I could not picture and who had their own small boats and went off in them by themselves – it meant nothing. I could never dive deep into those books and immerse myself.

But that was rare. I think it would be with most Reading Children. Reading is magic. Books are magic. It starts when we are shown picture books and realise there is another world beyond the everyday one we know. Once we can read ourselves, we live inside the magic. The only problem is that we have to emerge at the end of a book, and we don't want to leave and return to that dull domestic world we know. The only solution to that problem, of course, is that there is always the next book, and the next and there is bonus magic if it is another in a series we already love, so we are plunging back into a magic other world but one we already know. We feel a lift of the heart, a lurch of the stomach, when we find ourselves in it again.

When does it all stop? Because although Reading Children become Reading Adults, and I can become almost as immersed in a book now as I could at aged nine, it still is never quite the same. I don't think it has anything to do with adult duties and distractions – or only a little. We can carve out a whole afternoon or evening to read and plan not to be interrupted. Besides, we can just as easily be pulled up to the surface, when we are children, by 'Time for bed', 'Time for lunch', 'Time for homework', 'Go and wash your hands', 'Get your face out of that book and go outside for some fresh air'.

No, it starts when we have to do something WITH our books. Talk about them. Describe them. Recount the plot. Write an essay about them. And later, analyse, criticise, discuss. The magic world has a new purpose, a Gradgrind purpose, an examination purpose. It is a bit like being taken round the back of a puppet show to be shown how the strings work. A friend who adored the TV series *All Creatures Great and Small* was given the opportunity to watch some of the filming. The programmes were never the same for her again. The secrets were revealed. The set was just a set, the house only the facade of a house. The magic had been explained away.

I am certain that writers are formed in part by the books they have read and absorbed and it troubles me that not all writers or aspiring writers *are* Reading Writers. Increasingly, I meet creative writing students who do not read. They are ignorant of the best. They are often even ignorant of the worst. So how on earth can they want to write themselves? How do they know what it is all about? Read, read, read is the only advice I give, if asked. Read those writers who are better than you or I will ever be. In the end, that is the only way you will learn.

In *The Scarlet Tree*, the second volume of his fine and now underrated autobiography, Osbert Sitwell says that the writer, like the child, flourishes best in an atmosphere of affection and encouragement. Maybe that is all the writer needs, other than to be surrounded by books, to which she has open access. A Reading Child.

But writers have flourished in conditions of great adversity and discouragement. Maybe that's something to do with the stubbornness and sheer bloody-mindedness innate in some of us. Putting obstacles in the path of youthful ambition can have wonderful results in the opposite way from those intended. But only sometimes. Only sometimes.

———•○•———

THERE WAS A SNIPE by the river today.

———•○•———

DAVID'S ANNIVERSARY. Always remembered, with love. I was going to marry him. A turbulent affair was just coming right.

It was on such a beautiful early spring day as this that he went for his last walk, in the Gloucestershire countryside. Blackthorn. The first flush of leaves on the trees. Hazel catkins. Scurrying blackbirds, low in the hedgerows. And his churchyard, at Buckland, full of daffodils. He died in that church, alone, quietly, suddenly, quite unexpectedly, after having felt tired. He was forty-three. I was thirty.

David disapproved of purple patches, of ornate flourishes and unnecessary decoration, in music and in literature. He was right. Al Alvarez says it definitively in *The Writer's Voice*:

> *High style is the writer's equivalent of putting on airs and dropping names … What is sometimes passed off as 'fine writing' … is usually little more than a set of secondhand stylistic devices that cost the writer nothing and flatter the reader into believing that, through it, they have graduated into a better class of literature. Fine writing indulged for its own sake also projects the image of an exquisite sensibility exposing itself for admiration …*

Less is more. That does not mean bland, dull, flat. It means spare and elegant and lean, with every single word pulling its weight and, if it is not, it is redundant. Get rid of it.

It was Dr Johnson who said 'Read over your compositions, and where ever you meet with a passage which you think is particularly fine, strike it out.' It is a fine balance, though. Dickens, that master of literary oratory and thundering rhetorical prose, is the great exception to the rule.

I have always found it better not to read any contemporary fiction while writing it, because I can catch another writer's style like measles and the same applies to reading Dickens, whose cadences, so magnificent coming from him, in one's own prose appear bloated and pompous.

The Writer's Voice is short and packed with good things. Alvarez illuminates Donne, Coleridge, Sylvia Plath in a sentence or two as revelatory as a scalpel. Afterwards you read those writers yourself with a new and different view and understanding. And he is as good on novelists as he is on poets.

There are some writers for whom writing is a charm against an intolerable reality, and for them the differences between the lived facts and the imagined story are greatest when the two are almost identical. Jean Rhys, for example, had artistic imagination and no invention at all: she couldn't dream up situations she herself had not been in, the people in her stories were the people she knew, and a great deal of what she wrote in her diaries she rewrote in her novels.

Another moment to pause and wonder all over again whether this matters. If the reader does not know that Jean Rhys wrote her own life over and over again in her novels, but assumes all of it is indeed invention, does that make any difference? Transmuting the lived life into fiction, many years later, is as great a skill as imagining and inventing lives and characters and events. Does it make any difference to me to know what I know about Rhys and the way she worked? I can never completely make up my mind. I do know that what applies to much else applies to fiction – that it will all be the same in a hundred years time. With novels, make that two hundred.

APRIL

I ALWAYS TRY AN APRIL FOOL joke on Facebook and it is generally uncovered within seconds, but I did have one triumph a few years ago, when I said I could now reveal that I had been appointed to write the official biography of Her Majesty the Queen. The excited congratulations lasted until after noon, when I pointed people to the date. Most satisfying.

THE BLACKTHORN IS WHITENING the hedgerows, but the weather is having its joke this year. April often comes in with bitter winds and sometimes snow, too, so that we have 'a blackthorn winter'. This year, there is sunshine all the way. Warm sunshine.

NO HEDGEHOG YET. Just too cold. When we had our tortoise, Clarabel, we watched for her to emerge from about now and year after year she did – and then dived back under the covers again for another few weeks of snoozing. It was from Clarabel that I learned that a tortoise can distinguish between colours. If I put a tomato or a strawberry out on the grass she would trundle over for it. If I put out something green – lettuce or a few cabbage leaves – she might eat them when she came upon them but she did not make a beeline for them. She was the easiest animal companion ever, undemanding, enjoying a bit of company, but equally happy with solitude, requiring no walks or balls or squeaky toys. She was vegetarian, lived in harmony with everything else that shared the garden, and slept as deeply as a Moomin for half the year. When we sold the cottage to friends, we knew that we could not take her with us, as our new big garden would not have been safe for her for five minutes. We did not sell Clarabel to the new cottage owners, we gave her to them on permanent loan. They sent us a news bulletin on her twice a year and when she failed to emerge one final spring, they told us straight away, in a very kind and sensitive e-mail. Perfect.

———•○•———

I ALWAYS THINK of my rarely met but always loved friend, Miriam Margolyes, whenever I look along the Dickens shelves. She says that she was born to play Mrs Gamp, and her *Dickens' Women* show was a triumph. She has often suggested I should write something for her and at last I came up with an idea she loved. I will not say what it is, in case I can give it a new lease of life somewhere after all, but when an excited producer put it to the Head of Drama, that illustrious personage waved a hand. 'I don't do monologues.'

Lots of great stories about Miriam go round, all of them true. The most recent is about a trip to India. She and a group of theatre management folk were sitting in a resplendent hotel foyer when Miriam happened to see a woman come in through the doors to the reception desk. 'My God!' she said, in tones of great awe. 'Look! That is one of the most beautiful women I have seen in my entire life. Possibly *the* most beautiful woman.' Whereupon she leaped up, went over to the woman and said, 'I have to tell you that you are the most beautiful woman I have ever seen in my entire life. Who *are* you?'

The woman smiled a beautiful smile at her. 'Well, thank you! My name is Joan Baez.'

———•○•———

MOLES, MOLES, MOLES. They leave their neat soil mountains on the lawn. I refuse to have anyone trap or beat them to death, but I want to urge them to build their heaps in the field on the other side of the wall. I bought a dozen solar mole spikes – and they are not cheap. You stick one into the middle of a mole hill and, once charged up, it emits a sort of buzz or soft screech which hurts the moley ears and they flee. It worked a treat last year, but now the moles are back and preferring the lawn again. For a few days the moles ignore the spikes – maybe they have not taken in enough solar power to build up to full pitch. But then we have three sunny days and even from the kitchen I can hear the massed bands of mole deterrents tuning up.

They've gone! On the other side of the wall, in the field not the lawn, I see a little flotilla of freshly dug mole hills.

But I am keeping the solar spikes out in the sun to re-charge, just in case. The soil the moles dig up with their strong paws is very fine, if you sift it through your fingers. You can use it for seedlings straight away.

A lot of creatures live strange lives, and none stranger than the eel, but moles, in their solitary, industrious blindness, come close.

Moldy Warp features in the Little Grey Rabbit series of children's books by Alison Uttley. I sent the first one to Lila and, assuming that it would be a nice gentle bunny story, Jess began to read it to her at bed time – only to discover that it is about Little Grey Rabbit cutting off her own tail and giving it away.

———•○•———

I AM BACK to Edith Wharton.

What an extraordinary woman she was. I had never heard of her until someone told me they had been to see the film of *The Age of Innocence*. I am not one for film adaptations of novels, so I got the book instead, and from page one I was hooked, and went from that to *The House of Mirth* and *The Custom of the Country*. There was once a fat Penguin paperback containing all three, but of course they let that go out of print. The middle title is the masterpiece – but that is not to leave the others far behind.

I knew nothing about Wharton. I assumed these novels were all she had written, yet something was bumping about at the back of my mind. I discovered *Ethan Frome* and disliked it. Others think it a small work of genius, but there is something stark and cold about it and it did not ring true to me because it is set in rural America and, above all, Edith was a city woman. Still, it is regarded as a great short novel, so I am probably wrong.

The thing went on bumping about in my mind but there was no clue in any of the Old New York trio. I had to wait until I got back home and wandered from room to room, shelf to shelf, before coming upon what I did not know I was looking for. *The Ghost Stories of Edith Wharton*. I remembered them as soon as I opened the book, but the name had never connected in my mind with the author of *The House of Mirth*.

Her life was remarkable, especially for a woman of her time, but not knowing anything about her does not detract from the fiction because it is not autobiographical – though the Old New York she writes about was the one she and, to a greater extent, her parents knew so well. No, Edith Wharton is a fascinating woman because she is a fascinating woman. You could find much interest and enjoyment from reading all about her in the good biographies without reading a word of her fiction, and there are coffee table books about the gardens she created, and about her interior design, mainly but not only for her own houses in both America and France. That was unexpected. But there is more.

If you are born into an aristocracy of whatever country, you are an aristocrat for life. You are rooted in a society to which so many aspire to belong and which has formed your taste, manners, beliefs, assumptions, for good, no matter where else you may travel to or in what other country you may settle. It is important to remember this in order to realise just how extraordinary Edith Wharton's life turned out to be, and how unlike most of her own class she became. Yet she remained one of the aristocrats of Old New York in spite of leaving America for Europe often – she worked out that she had crossed the Atlantic more than sixty times – eventually to remain. Through family marriages, she had connections with all New York society. But she was one of those children who are unhappy not only in their own families and backgrounds, but even in their own skin. She was destined to fulfil herself as an adult but her early years were unhappy, because she was bright and noticed things, and because her mother was cold towards her. She loved her father deeply, but he was a weak man who vacillated when she asked him to stand up for her against his wife, who even forbade EW from reading novels until she was married.

Her first marriage was less than happy because her husband had inherited what we would now called clinical depression. But they established houses, Edith began to write and, eventually, they went abroad for the first time. It was her awakening. She took an intelligent and passionate interest in European houses and interior, and in gardens, which, together with her increasingly successful writing, were to remain her lifelong study and delight.

The House of Mirth was the first of her novels to become a best-seller. After that, she, who had always lived prosperously thanks to a private income from family trusts, now became rich from her own work.

When she and Teddy Wharton were eventually divorced, she re-married, though not before she had fallen in love with another man and begun to engage with the great literary figures of the day, most especially Henry James. Her novels are often compared with his and he became her staunch admirer, but whereas his fiction became denser and more difficult to read as he grew older, Wharton's was always more straightforward. She was a great student of human nature. She understood women, but she also knew an unnerving amount about men. She writes about social ambition, social aspiration, social climbing – the nuances of society, and about the cruelty with which it can appear to accept, only to exclude and cast off, any who are not within its charmed circle by right of birth, or at least of marriage. The story of Lily Bart, in *The House of Mirth*, is about society, but essentially it is a deeply felt human tragedy.

Already, then, Edith Wharton lived a full, varied and even adventurous life. But more and more surprises were to come. She was living in Paris when the First World War broke out and very soon afterwards, in August 1914, she opened a sewing workroom for thirty unemployed women, feeding them and paying them a modest wage. The thirty soon doubled to sixty and their work was in demand. She established a hostel for Belgian refugees, and organised the Children of Flanders Rescue Committee which eventually looked after almost a thousand child refugees who had fled their towns after they had been bombed by the German army. With her friend Walter Berry she even travelled by car to the war zone, coming within a short distance of the trenches, in order to see at first hand what conditions were like. She compiled and edited a book in aid of war victims, prised money for them out of wealthy Americans and was awarded the Légion d'honneur by the French government. And all this time she continued to write novels, essays, stories – and kept up a large correspondence.

She never returned to live in America. France was her adopted country and she remained there, though travelled about, mainly to Italy. She went on studying European interior and garden design, she wrote an important book about the former, and created wonderful gardens at her own homes.

Who would have expected this woman, this fine, perceptive, quintessentially American member of an elite society, as well as a major novelist, to have been so involved with and successful at helping war victims so practically in another country, and to have such an eye and taste for two very different forms of design?

I take down the best biography of Edith Wharton – by Hermione Lee – which I have had on the shelf since its publication, and skim through it again. Worth knowing, is Mrs Wharton, even without the fiction. And of how many writers can that be said? Yes, the Brontës; yes, Dickens and a few others.

She is inspiring, I think as I put *The Age of Innocence* down on the table, having finished it yet again. She encourages one to do so much more, be so much more.

Still, in the end, the novels have it. They have enriched me over thirty years. I can't say that about every book I have ever opened.

———•○•———

WENT TO PICK UP a prescription. The doctors' surgery is across a meadow from the steam train station (there are some diesels, too). The line runs from Holt to Sheringham, via Weybourne – and from it there are beautiful views of coast and sea. As with all of these privately run, manned-by-volunteers lines, there are all manner of special steam events – the Santa Train, the annual 1940s weekend. But it is good to travel on an ordinary day, to get a real sense of how steam was all through my childhood. The super Scarborough to Whitby line was my favourite – that track was taken up, though there are one or two nostalgia tea-rooms where station platforms used to be. The train across the North York Moors from Pickering and Goathland still runs as a tourist attraction, though, and it is a joyous sight to see it trundling across the horizon, steam puffing out into the summer sky. I loved travelling by train as a child and I still do, but steam to those of us who knew it well had an especial charm – though not so much for the railway-men, who mostly died of lung diseases caused by the smoke and coal tar, or were old at fifty, backs broken from shovelling the coal.

I remember my friend Damian whenever I see a steam train. Damian worked as a volunteer on the Tallylyn railway, and as a signalling expert for his day job. We used to discuss trains and train lines all the time, and little else – and we were in our twenties.

The last time I heard anyone refer to the old railway companies by their nicknames was in the 1970s when a friend said he was off to watch the cricket but was not taking his car. 'I shall go by the Slow and Dirty.' That was the Somerset & Dorset Joint Railway. LNER (London & North Eastern Railway) was Late and Never Early. LMS (London, Midland & Scottish) was Late, Mouldy and Slow. And of course the GWR (Great Western) was God's Wonderful Railway.

Nostalgia is a delightful thing, if biased. I don't think everything has gone downhill since the end of steam, though I am inclined to take that view re. Beeching and his axe to branch lines. (Another nod to Flanders and Swann and *The Slow Train* …) John Betjeman's poems about railways remind one of how much was lost …

Rumbling under blackened girders, Midland, bound for
   Cricklewood,
Puffed its sulphur to the sunset where that Land of Laundries
   stood.

It isn't possible to read those words from 'Parliament Hill Fields' without hearing JB's voice reciting it, just as for 'April is the cruellest month', the opening of *The Waste Land*, I always hear in my head the version read by T. S. Eliot himself, though his voice was dry and dull, whereas Betjeman's was rich and fruity. Both were shot through with melancholy.

With railways in my mind, I picked up a paperback called *On the Slow Train Again* by Michael Williams, and here is a whole section on the stations, old and new, of North Norfolk … Cromer, Sheringham – from whence still runs the Bittern Line slowly to Norwich – West Runton, Weybourne.

And here is Candida Lycett Green, John Betjeman's daughter and one of my dearest, most missed of friends, on Cromer:

Cromer is a magical place… all red pantile roofs, cedar trees, pinnacled Victorian and Edwardian houses, flamboyant verandas on the edge of the old town … It was the arrival of the railway in 1877 which finally put the gilt on Cromer's gingerbread.

Candida wrote that in 2010 and Cromer is still magical, though very much an acquired taste, as my mother said of gin.

———•○•———

THERE HAS BEEN A VOGUE in the past decade or so for pastiche Victorian detective novels set in and on and around the railways, but railway poems have been written for far longer. Such as C. L. Graves' 'Railway Rhymes':

When books are pow'rless to beguile
And papers only stir my bile,
For solace and relief I flee
To Bradshaw or the ABC
And find the best of recreations
In studying the names of stations.

And then of course there is Edward Thomas's 'Adlestrop'. I used to live a few miles away from the village, and often make a detour just to see the famous station sign which stands on the green and the one line that always came into my head was 'all the birds/Of Oxfordshire and Gloucestershire' – Adlestrop stands on the border between the two counties. Another melancholy poem, though. Is there a jolly railway train one?

We learned W. H. Auden's *Night Mail* by heart at school:

This is the night mail crossing the border,
Bringing the cheque and the postal order.

And Eliot's 'Skimbleshanks, The Railway Cat' is briskly jolly. But perhaps the subject as a whole is too redolent of partings and long distant memories. Though with arrivals and meetings and reunions, too. I travel to London from King's Lynn, via Ely – with the cathedral, 'The Ship of the Fens', rearing up in view – and Cambridge, though you catch no glimpse of dreaming spires from the station.

HM the Queen spends Christmas, and the whole of January, at Sandringham, in Norfolk, and travels up here from London by train in mid-December. She sits in the front first class coach with her detective, and the rest of the train fills up as normal. At King's Lynn, the stationmaster is waiting – and there is always a photograph of him in his best suit and beaming with pride – to meet and greet her and escort her to her car. She walks a few yards up the platform and exits through the side gate, while we all pile off behind her cheerfully and go to run our tickets through the machine at the barrier. I say 'we' because I have travelled on her train and there is the minimum of fuss, which suits everyone. The stationmaster gets his annual moment in the sun and we other passengers feel a flush of superiority that we have just shared the same journey as the Queen. And if the train had broken down, as it sometimes does, she would have got to enjoy the fun of that, too.

The buffet at King's Lynn is over a hundred years old and still has its original façade and doors. Inside isn't very modern either. They do a great bacon butty, hot and freshly cooked, for the early commuters. I wish the Queen would pop in there some time to say hello, even if she passes on the butty. Apparently they always know in there when she is coming, because the sniffer dogs come in beforehand. (Possibly also for the bacon butties.) Whereas most station buffets are stocked with mass-produced plastic food, ours has homemade sandwiches and hot toast. It is always busy in the run-up to the hourly London train, especially in the early morning, but it goes quiet in between, so it might still be fit for a *Brief Encounter* at the table in the corner.

———•○•———

JUST OCCASIONALLY THE BARE-FACED cheek of some people does stop me in my tracks. Letter from a woman saying she has a 'truly fantastic' idea for a ghost story but, having tried several times to write it herself, she realises it needs 'a more expert hand'. So if she tells it to me, and I write it, she reckons we have a best-seller. She would give me a percentage. And if this one succeeds, she has more ideas where this one came from.

There is really no possible answer. So I haven't.

———•○•———

IN CORNWALL, THE SWALLOWS had arrived by 2 April and were already busily nesting in their cliff holes. They were seen on a Devon telegraph wire on 8 April and by me on a Norfolk wire on the tenth. And so they move up country.

In Cornwall I saw a white throat. None here yet, but they are quite elusive.

On a walk round the lakes at Pensthorpe nature reserve yesterday we saw the first ducklings, eight little bumble bees clustered round their mother. As soon as we neared, she gathered them all very close and ushered them towards the water but didn't actually plop in. Meanwhile, the drake lifted his wings in a hostile gesture, warning us away – traditional role assignment, though plenty of male birds and animals share in the nest-sitting and child-feeding.

POPPING INTO A LIVELY TWITTER exchange between a group of writers, I found the traditional favourite subjects under discussion. That genius American teller and illustrator of strange tales, Edward Gorey, wrote a book called *The Unstrung Harp*, which features an aspiring writer called Mr Earbrass. When Mr Earbrass goes to a literary party he finds that 'The talk deals with disappointing sales, inadequate publicity, more than inadequate royalties, idiotic or criminal reviews, others' declining talent, and the unspeakable horror of the literary life'.

I would add the talk about what utter agony and ceaseless toil writing is, but otherwise nothing changes.

ACCORDING TO A. E. HOUSMAN, 'Loveliest of trees, the cherry now …' And so it is. I have not missed many things from our twenty-five years in the Cotswold farmhouse, but each April I miss, with a hollow in my heart, the four and a half acres of cherry trees I planted on the rising meadow there. Once, when I wandered down through their rows under a full moon, the barn owl came gliding down beside me on silent wings. Magic always touches us when unbidden and least expected. In spite of what the fairy tales and Harry Potter tell us, we cannot conjure it up for ourselves. But it is not entirely true that magical worlds can only be entered when we are children, and that adults worlds are grey and full of facts and plain speaking. Any tree in full creamy blossom, any moonlit night, can open the door of memory for me, on to the cherry orchard.

I have heard Housman called sentimental and worse. But what does that mean? It means he has the power to awaken a response in us, the power to move us.

Now, of my threescore years and ten,
Twenty will not come again,
And take from seventy springs a score,
It only leaves me fifty more.

And since to look at things in bloom
Fifty springs are little room,
About the woodlands I will go
To see the cherry hung with snow.

Is a poet's power to move us to do with use of language only? What else, other than choice of subject, that awakens an answering response in the reader even before a line has been read? 'Ode on the Death of a Child' has a head start by comparison with one, say, 'On Military Might'.

W. H. Auden's poems are sometimes witty, often thought-provoking and can also be moving, but do they make tears prick behind the eyes? 'Stop all the clocks ...' may, but probably because of context.

Eliot? Clever, thought-provoking, complex, knotty – but moving? I have not been emotionally disturbed by a T. S. Eliot poem. Yet some of them get right under the skin. *Four Quartets* has great solemnity and some phrases provoke an intense personal sense of nostalgia.

Perhaps it is a mite too easy to be upset by Housman. The rhyming helps him. Rhyme always does. The subject matter – the deaths of young men in war, their beautiful English home county and countryside, Englishness in general, youth lost, old age approaching too soon. Easy to cry at any of these. Does that make him a glib poet? Slick? Sentimental? I am not sure. He himself famously said that he judged true poetry by whether or not the hairs on your chin bristle if one repeats it while shaving. That has been sneered at a lot over the years. But it has something to do with that ... On the other hand, that probably never happens to anyone reading Milton, Pope or Dryden – mighty poets all.

But Alexander McCall Smith has made me take a long, close look at W. H. Auden again, the poet I learned so much of for A Level, whose poems I have never forgotten. McCall Smith's small book *What W. H. Auden Can Do for You* illuminates the poetry in a highly individual way and clarifies it, too, so that we read him with new eyes. And that, surely, is the best achievement of any literary critic. His final paragraph is one any author would be humbled to read about himself – and which justifies the existence any work of literature, poetry or prose, as well as the existence of its maker.

I have learned so much from this poet. I have been transported by his words. My life has been enriched by his language. I have stopped and thought, and thought, over so many of his lines. He can be with us in every part of our lives, showing us how rich life can be, and how precious.

Indeed, say that of any poet, or novelist, who has been so essential to you, has helped form the person you are.

Who is my W. H. Auden?

I have a few art books. Not a random assortment about Monet/Manet/Van Gogh/Rubens/Michelangelo, which I would probably never look at, just a selection about painters who appeal to me in a way different from simple admiration or awe, though I am inarticulate about art so usually I cannot explain why.

I have loved David Hockney's work ever since I first saw a limited edition print of his for sale in 1965 and wanted it more than almost anything I have ever wanted, other than my first bike. It was a drawing of tulips in a vase and now I know his work much better I would see that it could have been by no one else but DH. At the time, I just gazed and longed and longed and gazed. It was £60, and I had no money, let alone £60 to buy a work of art. I yearned and coveted that picture. I dreamed about it. The next time I walked past the small local gallery, it had gone.

I have regretted ever since that I didn't beg, borrow or steal to buy it, but in the sober light of day I know I could not have had it and even if I had I would probably have had to sell it five years down the line when I was even poorer.

Still, there are the David Hockney books on the special shelf in the sitting room, for just one row of very tall books.

I often go in there, not necessarily to sit, just to look for something mislaid maybe, and then I take one of them down and look closely at a few pages of pictures for ten minutes or so. Always rewarding. It is also a plus that Hockney came from Bridlington – not Scarborough, but the next best thing and only a few miles down the coast. There was always a rivalry: 'Are you from/which do you like best, Scarborough or Brid?' A lot can ride on the answer.

The other half of the shelf is taken up by books by and about John Piper, whom I knew, together with and inseparable from his wife Myfanwy, and who were such a significant part of my life for nearly thirty years.

It was in Scarborough that I first saw a painting by John, when I was a child and we went to the house called Woodend – in those days part museum, part art gallery, part tea room, with one room devoted to the Sitwell family, whose home this had once been. John Piper had painted the other Sitwell family seat, Renishaw Hall in Derbyshire, and the pictures hung in that room, as did others by him, several of which were of Windsor Castle. They were commissioned by King George VI and painted in dark colours. When the King first saw them, he said, 'You seem to have very bad luck with your weather, Mr Piper.'

I can hear John's voice repeating the story now. I hear his voice often – distinctive, slightly posh – as so many of his generation's voices were then. (He was born in Epsom, Surrey, and was not posh at all, just safely middle class, but the fact remained.) He punctuated his talk with lovely words like 'jolly', as in 'jolly nice of you to come/say so/bring it'.

Overnight stays in the Pipers' farmhouse at Fawley Bottom in south Oxfordshire were very special. The house was special. The garden was special. The studio was special. The place had a magic I have never known anywhere else, because of its setting, what it contained, its atmosphere, but most of all its creators.

I lived in Leamington Spa, so I would drive down the old road (the M40 was not yet finished) in my battered Mini, feeling excitement with each signpost bringing me nearer. The dual carriageway towards Henley-on-Thames. A left turn and a winding road through the hills above it, above the river, dipping a bit, rising some more, and then a sharp left into the gateway and there it was. An Oxfordshire stone farmhouse, with a big barn to the right, converted as John's studio for his larger paintings. Pull up in front of the kitchen door which was the one used for all entrances and exits, and John would emerge, tall, thin and with a slightly stiff walk, like a crane. He was one of the most welcoming, hospitable and polite of men, always took my bag and told me it was jolly nice to see me, jolly nice of me to come, asked about the drive, and so on into the kitchen, where Myfanwy would almost always be, apparently cooking, in that pieces of meat or fish seemed to be slipped casually into the Aga, to emerge a few hours later as a perfectly cooked dish.

Myfanwy was a natural and instinctive cook and, long before it became fashionable, always used local produce, real meat, veg from the garden, other things from farmers or cheesemakers around. And it was far less easy to find those things then.

I never understood what people meant by a Celtic face until I saw Myfanwy. She was Welsh, though had no accent. Her face is impossible to describe and did not always photograph well. It was startling, remarkable, interesting, intelligent, bony, but not hawk-like, as John's was. Her hair hung short and straight, she did not wear make-up, but she wore nice frocks and very high heels which showed off good legs, and unusual necklaces. I was a little frightened of her as I never was of John. She could be scathing, her wit and scorn could occasionally be caustic, but she was kind. They were friends who offered friendship as it is most valued – sympathetic, understanding, sometimes bracing, occasionally disapproving. But strong. Reliable. If you were in a mess, trouble, in the midst of sadness or strife, you could go to them and feel stronger, and warmed by affection and good humour.

I always slept in the Book Room, which was literally that, dark, comfortable, ever-interesting. You only had to look round, reach out a hand to a shelf, to find treasures, and often signed treasures by old friends. The 1920s and 1930s and 1940s, poetry, fiction, topography, France, Venice, art, John's own books, complete Shell Guides to Britain which he produced with John Betjeman, runs of magazines – *Horizon*, the *London Magazine*, catalogues from galleries, often of John's own exhibitions. I could have spent days in there, looking and reading.

Dinner. John changed into a different jacket … maybe a velvet one, and one of his amazing shirts with broad stripes in vivid colours, and a Missoni tie or a French cravat. Myfanwy changed, too, into a rather sexy dress, usually in a softer or even sombre colour. She always looked good but John was the dandy. If it was winter, he would have lit the fire, having already fetched in logs and laid it earlier, and picked the vegetables, too. Their vegetable garden was like no other and they grew almost everything from seed. Then he would fetch up the right bottle of wine for the food, from the cellar, and open it, and light the candles. I have never seen candlesticks like theirs. They were white china, absolutely straight and plain and square. I have seen many a white candlestick since but always with some curlicue or roundness or decoration or twist of the stem. I wish I had thought to ask where they came from, but I suspect it would have been from France, to which they travelled often. I have postcards of his from various French towns, usually of churches, and from Italy, usually Venice. When he drove Benjamin Britten and Peter Pears all the way there, Myfanwy and Ben in the back talking about her libretto for his opera of *Death in Venice*, John sent me a card from somewhere en route. 'Car and passengers behaving very well so far.'

After the meat, the salad, the fruit and the cheese – Myf did not do puddings, though sometimes there might be a fruit tart, brought home from a French patisserie in London after a day trip. And then there would be another glass of wine and the smell of the wood smoke and the candles and John would play the piano. Jazz. Old music hall tunes. Twenties numbers. A bit of Chopin, just occasionally. In summer, the door was open on to the garden.

The small studio was a late addition to the house, converted out of a barn at the end. It had deeply comfortable black leather sofas, with pots of brushes and china paint dishes around, portfolios of John's prints, new pictures on easels, and jugs, bowls and dishes from his very successful foray into pottery. A French 'Tortoise' stove. Smells of oil paint and turps and more wood smoke. And talk, while classical music played. Talk about people and places and ideas and politics and families and the Church and churches – John was a passionate Church of England churches man and on the Oxford diocesan board for their preservation and upkeep for many years. He painted just about every one in the county, as well as elsewhere, in Wales, all over France. He is buried in the churchyard of one of the most modestly typical English churches, at Fawley, where he was a churchwarden and took the collection every Sunday.

They had known so many of the painters and poets of their day. There was always a good story about someone or other. Someone had gone to lunch bearing a bottle of champagne, which neither of them liked. Myfanwy gave it a look. 'Graham Greene always liked *fizzy* drinks.'

I lost close touch with them for some time, not after my marriage and my first daughter, but a year or so later when I was focused on having a second child and kept failing and could think of nothing else. During that time, John and Myfanwy's granddaughter Lucy, who lived near to them, was killed in a road accident, beside which horror even the premature birth and subsequent death of my own infant seemed a small grief. But they read about it, from the announcement in the paper, and wrote and offered love and a place to stay which was safe and familiar if ever we needed it. A healing place.

It strikes me now that Fawley Bottom, and the Pipers' life there, was exactly that. After a stressful day and a drive down, perhaps in the dark and teeming rain, an evening there, dinner, music, talk and a night in the Book Room, breakfast with Myfanwy's homemade bread, one felt renewed and healed either from trivial difficulties or major ones.

John suffered the cruellest of last years in the grip of Alzheimer's. His funeral was as perfect and right as one can ever be, with John's favourite flowers, giant sunflowers, on his coffin and a bent, distraught but brave Myfanwy, supported on either sides by her son and grandson, as she dropped one of them into the grave. She had lost one son, Edward, their eldest, lost a beloved grand-daughter, and now she was saying farewell to her beloved John.

She lived on at Fawley Bottom into her nineties, still working on librettos, still seeing family, and so many friends, though the evenings at the Aga in her stilettos, evenings cooking and drinking wine and laughing and talking, were long gone and she was lovingly looked after rather than being the one in charge.

I went to visit her the year before she died. She made tea, there was a homemade cake. We wandered down the garden, which was still a garden, still with vegetables and flowers, but less tended, a shadow of its old self.

Myf was old and frail but still interested in everything, still lively, still with shrewd eyes and that short laugh full of meaning.

I drove away knowing I would not see her again. I said goodbye to her, to the house, the garden, John's studio, still as he had last used and left it, laying down the brush he no longer recognised, the paints he did not understand. I said goodbye to years of friendship, merriment, succour, music, good food, good wine, affection, in that healing place. And to those white candlesticks.

MAY

THE KIDS ARE ALL RIGHT. They are straightforward. I tell them, in a firm but friendly way, that I am happy to answer questions but I won't do their homework and can't do their exams for them. I can be straight with them, and they take it. But with the aspiring writers I have to tread carefully, for fear of bruising feelings, causing a set-back, breaking frail egos. I have to remember how generous and encouraging people were to me. It matters.

But. But, but, but. I wonder what they expect. What do they want? It isn't always riches. Facts have penetrated from all the statistics put out by the Royal Society of Literature and the *Bookseller* and the books page commentators.

What did I want? To 'be' a writer. To be published. To see my book(s) in hardback on shelves. To have readers. To be understood by readers. To be praised. To be allowed to go on writing and writing and having to do nothing else.

Is it the same now? Yes, I guess so. It has just got so much harder. Yet in some ways perhaps easier, too. Every new book jostles for attention and review space and shelf space and reader space with hundreds of others each month. Each week. Maybe when I began it was only dozens.

I trot out the old phrases. You need application. You need to read. You need to want it.

You need luck. Talent. More luck.

See if you can spend a year not writing and then ask yourself if you still want to do it.

I don't think I am ever much help. If you're going to do it, you will.

'If it's meant to be.' Is there any more to it than that?

I say it all again anyway. Then I think, who am I? I actually only know what I have learned for myself and that probably only applies to me. I write in fragments, more often than not … I don't sit for four or six hours, and I never get up and produce hundreds or thousands of consecutive sentences. I did once, but only because of limited time available in which to get anything down at all before homework or exam revision or the baby's crying or the children's supper called. I suspect my natural mode is the one I write in now, which is a bit here, a bit there. I notice that the daughter who writes does that, too – she can write a scene or two on a train, or while waiting for the pot to boil. A friend of hers recently lamented never being able to find three days without interruption in which to get going on her second novel. Maybe she never will. Maybe she will have to be more ruthless in carving out that time, or learn to use an hour to maximum advantage. Everyone is different, there are no rules, we all create our own way of doing it.

I say all this, too.

I am always tempted to ask, '*Why* do you want to be a writer?' Though most often they have more or less told me that already. But why the 'Why'? One never asks, 'Why do you read?' There is no shame in not really knowing about the writing, in saying just, 'I just know I love writing.' For myself, I say, 'Because I can' and 'Because I am otherwise unemployable'. And 'Because I have done it for the last seventy years and I can no more imagine myself not writing than I can not breathing. And the consequence of both might well be the same.'

Do people want to paint in this way, or sculpt, or compose, or dance? Some do, but nowhere near as many, simply because of the technical challenges and requirements. Everyone can write, ergo everyone can write a book.

The older I get the more divided I become. On the one hand, let everyone write a book who wants to, and have it published, the more the merrier. On the other, there are too many books in the world already, and too many new books published, making claims on people's reading time and purses and on shelf space and …

Maybe there is no answer. That is true of quite a few things, after all.

———•○•———

ALAN JUDD. Most people know him as a spy story maestro, author of the Charles Thorogood series – A *Breed of Heroes, Legacy, Uncommon Enemy, Inside Enemy.* Good spy stories are hard to come by and probably harder to write. I have occasionally toyed with doing one but have always been deterred by the riches of those already available and the long shadow of John le Carré. Once you have read the George Smiley novels, what more do you need?

But I had never heard of Alan Judd, and he had not written his spy stories, when my then French publisher asked me what I thought of a novel called *The Devil's Own Work* by Alan Judd and proffered her opinion that it was a work of genius. Others from the French book world who sat around the table nodded in agreement. So I bought *The Devil's Own Work.*

She was right. It is a fine novella. It is quite short, impeccably written, immaculately structured, beautifully shaped. It is by turn enigmatic, touching, frightening, ambiguous, but never less than impressive. It more than nods to Ford Madox Ford's *The Good Soldier* – hardly surprising, given that Judd wrote a prize-winning biography of Ford. It is not like that masterpiece in subject matter or setting, but there is something in the tone, and in the way the narrator tells his story. There is nothing wrong with that. We all beg, borrow and steal from one another, much of the time quite unconsciously. We read and remember other people's novels, dive down deep into that place from which our own books derive, and are transmuted, possibly over many years. We are not copying. But no book is an island, entire of itself.

I have just re-read *The Devil's Own Work*, wondering if I would still be impressed. Sometimes a book has its day and, although of course it does not change, the reader does, as a result of having read better things, or new tastes having come to the fore, or fashions in literature having moved on. Other novels seem to have improved, usually because we have matured as readers, our imaginations have expanded and we understand new literary approaches, sometimes because of life events which have opened us up to a new emotional awareness and understanding. It really does not matter. I can still enjoy and appreciate *Alice in Wonderland*, whereas *Fifth Form at Malory Towers* can yield me nothing more.

The Devil's Own Work is on one level a horror story, about a Faustian pact, and there are some suitably dark, menacing moments, but it is also a shrewd comment on literary fiction and writers puffed up beyond their true value. Once you grasp both aspects, the book acquires further richness, but even at first reading it is a fine story – and one of the best written of novellas.

It is still in print and I still recommend it.

And that's another thing – the perils of recommending books.

———•O•———

HAS MAY EVER BEEN SO COLD? Eight degrees here today and the wind made it feel like minus 8. But there have been other Mays like this. The year I was married, our wedding day, 23 April (Shakespeare and St George), was very warm and sunny. The day we had our wedding party, a month later, it was no more than 10, windy and wild and wet. During the May Bank Holiday weekend of 1984, when I was in hospital, I lay looking at rain being dashed against the ward windows. Nurses, coming on and off duty, were soaked and frozen.

So this weather is nothing new but it still feels unseasonal. The cuckoo has shut up, the swallows appeared and vanished again and the lilac is being bent and bashed about.

Huddled indoors, looking as ever for something different to read, I ran my fingers along a shelf and stopped at *How to Disappear*. I seem to have three copies in three different versions with three different covers. Even as I took one down and went to the sofa with it, I had already gone back to a warm Cotswold summer ten years ago – warm but with intermittent monsoons – and the time that Duncan came to stay in the flat at one end of our barn.

Duncan. Duncan Fallowell, author of *How to Disappear* and other brilliant, eccentric, quirky books by a man who Has Adventures. Duncan has adventures because he goes about looking for them – an admirable trait, though one which I have never shared.

His adventures are sometimes self-sought – like those he met with in New Zealand. He wrote about them in *Going as Far as I Can*. Then there was his trip *To Noto* – Noto is a place in Sicily to which he drove from London. Duncan drives everywhere. His adventures are sometimes topographical, sometimes architectural, but mostly they are of the human sort. I have never known anyone who has bumped by chance into such an extraordinary array of people, simply because that is how he sets his compass. He walks into a bar and the only other man drinking a pint there turns out to be a former lover of Evelyn Waugh … that sort of thing.

I have never known anyone else like Duncan. One doesn't. In his youth he was one of the handsomest men ever, with louche, sexy, decadent good looks. Now, older, he still has more than a shadow of them, because he is slender, but also young in outlook, up for anything, inquisitive, excitable. But thank goodness, he is not 'forever young' in that irritating Peter Pan way.

He shocks me and worries me and delights me by turn, and he is one of the most disciplined and meticulous writers I have ever known. He makes me feel slovenly. He takes infinite pains.

He ought to be better known and more widely celebrated than he is, because he is incapable of writing a dull sentence. When you plunge into a DF book you set off on an adventure yourself. He is an urban man, a London man, in spite of needing some quiet time in remoter places, and you don't go to him for descriptions of wildlife and the natural world. You go for two things, apart from the adventure – for towns and cities, the manmade landscape, and for people. At one time he wrote a lot of profiles for colour supplements and magazines – pop stars, actors, writers, even aristocrats. There is a great one in *To Noto* of Mick Jagger.

His piece about a visit to Sacheverell Sitwell towards the end of his life, at his home in Northamptonshire, is one of the best ever about that amazing, lovable man. Duncan conjures up both the man and his surroundings so that I felt I was sitting there with Sachie all over again.

Duncan is a perspicacious and clear-eyed profiler because he gets to know his subject, in so far as that subject will allow him. When one does, the result is very rewarding. I wish he could have interviewed the late Diana, Princess of Wales, because he understood her, he knew what made her tick and he also hit the spot, in so far as anyone ever has, about exactly why she was so loved and why her death, funeral and the whole period surrounding them were like nothing else before or after. Almost. Because he himself does not really understand it. Who did? He kept haunting Kensington Palace, looking at the flowers as they piled higher and higher, and at the people bringing them, breathing in the atmosphere, being saddened and moved and trying to answer all the questions. Nothing else has brought that time twenty years ago back to me as Duncan does.

Perhaps he would rather be known as a novelist. Maybe he thinks he is best at that. But he is best as a unique traveller, spotter of idiosyncrasies and eccentrics, at putting his finger on the pulse of a place. I have never wanted to go New Zealand, and after reading his book about it I want to go even less. I know why, too. But *To Noto* makes me want to go to Sicily, as well as afraid of ever doing so. It was Sachie Sitwell who gave him his send-off there – Sachie, another lover of strange places, oddities, curiosities in the great human museum of the weird. They had something in common. But Sachie was a lover of Venice, and Duncan is a Venice hater – which is quite ridiculous, principally because he has never been. He has set his face against it like a child who will never eat a banana just because he has been told it is delicious and he will absolutely love it, and so is determined he will loathe it.

We had some good talks, the summer that he came to stay, sitting in the garden at dusk and after dark, over glasses of wine, the puppy at our feet, the cats somewhere about, silent shadows. And the owls in the long barn. The flat in which Duncan was staying was at one end of the barn and at the other was an open balcony, in which the barn owl had nested. Several young owls had fledged and at night they made a strange hissing noise, and the hissing ran right along the wooden beam into the bedroom where Duncan slept, head against the same beam, so that he woke, ter-rified of the ghostly sound and quite unable to discover what it was. He did not come over to the house in his terror then but early morning saw him ashen-faced, at our door. I explained about the baby owls, finding it quite funny. I don't think he did.

I have been re-reading my way through his books, moving from one to the next in no particular order. There is renewed surprise and fresh interest that jumps out from every other page.

He takes your breath away with some of his images: 'French electricity pylons are more like people than English ones. They have little thalidomide arms, large heads, erect terrier ears.'

He is very perceptive about people as they really are, not as they present themselves. He read one of Dirk Bogarde's volumes of autobiography and got the man exactly right. 'Beneath the care-fully casual exterior it was all terribly uptight. Bogarde says that his great quality is charm. It isn't. It is sadness. An aura of extreme emotional vulnerability gives depth even to his trashiest roles.'

Spot on, as when he says that Bogarde was 'the finest British screen actor alive' (as he was then).

Bogarde could never ever admit to his own homosexuality. He could never see that it was clear as crystal to the rest of the world. Of course, that was partly the times in which he lived. But in the course of the research for the book, Duncan also went to see Sir Angus Wilson and his partner Tony Garrett, who had just moved to France, after decades in rural Suffolk. They went because, as Angus said, 'I do find all that hypocrisy about homosexuality and so on very hard to swallow. They were quite awful in Suffolk when Tony was forced out of his job as a very good probation officer, saying how much everyone liked him but really he couldn't be allowed to continue in the circumstances – just because he didn't hide our relationship.'

Yet Angus was in many ways a traditional, even conventional Englishman, and one of his times, too. He and Bogarde were poles apart. Angus was camp. Dirk tried his damnedest never to appear so.

Not long after their difficult and stressful move to France, disaster struck Angus and Tony, when they discovered that French law does not allow anyone not related by blood or marriage to inherit an estate. It has to go down in a particular order of relativity: spouse, parents, elder son and then other sons, then daughters, male cousins, female, and so on and so on until a fourteenth cousin three times removed may be reached. But a 'partner', hetero or homosexual, of however many years, gets nothing.

In panic, because by now Angus was ill, they fled back to England. The strain of all this can have done nothing to help his physical, let alone mental and emotional state.

But before any of this happened, Duncan Fallowell got an after-noon with them when they were still moving into their new place in St-Rémy-de-Provence, and he had tea and sugar-meringues 'glued together with jam', of which the Knight had a whole box, most of which he demolished with gusto, getting icing sugar all over himself without a care.

It isn't easy, at least for me, to have a 'books read' conversation with Duncan, though. I ask if he has read X or Y. 'No – my tastes are avant-garde.' He is the only person I know who would say that. I offer to send him the Patrick Melrose novels by Edward St Aubyn because I think he would 'get' them. But he refuses.

———•○•———

THE CENTRAL HEATING is back on. Hirundines seem to have returned to Africa even before their nests are full.

———•○•———

WHEN I AM WRITING CRIME NOVELS, I do not read any. It is all too easy to lift someone's idea inadvertently. Not the big idea – there are only so many of those in crime fiction, as in any other. No, it's the small things. And the setting. And what Jeeves called 'the psychology of the individual'. Val McDermid's DCI Carol Jordan and profiler Tony Hill, with their smooth professional rela-tionship and roller coaster personal one, are a great fictional pairing and having a profiler who is not a cop, and so is not so tied by police rules, works particularly well. I have never watched the television adaptations but the books are absorbing and intriguing, though the graphic violence gets to me sometimes.

I read three on the trot recently, after which I tried going back to

P. D. James. The later Adam Dalgliesh novels still reverberate but her early books seem a bit simplistic now. She learned on the job, as we all should, though it's surprising how many don't.

What a good, nice woman PDJ was. The *Spectator* gave me a lunch when I was seventy, to which I could invite whom I liked, and I asked Phyllis, though I hesitated beforehand, not expecting her to come, as she was ninety by then and, I assumed, frail. Not a bit of it. If she was less steady on her feet than the last time I had seen her, her mind was still razor sharp, and her conversation lively and challenging. She didn't duck the difficult topics. It was a joy to have her there, especially as it was the last time I saw her. Always ask.

She was very good at character, and at settings. I tired of her poet detective after a time, but her murderers were always complex individuals. The best of the novels are set in Suffolk, which she knew so well (and, after those, London and Oxford). She made such good use of the coast, of the river Thames, the churches and lanes and nooks and crannies of Oxford. One always walks there with her – and is always looking over one's shoulder. She is far better at Oxford than anyone else I have read and I wish she had set more of her books there.

Of the early novels, I think *A Shroud for a Nightingale* stands up best, but it is some years since I read it last. I must dig it out before I move on to another novelist. I have jags on one writer. I suppose many addicted readers do.

———•○•———

ANOTHER READING JAG, Ian Fleming/James Bond, but, after reading five in a row, I find only two that really satisfy in anything other than a 'slips down like ice cream' sort of way. *Casino Royale* can be read any number of times, even simply for the great Texas Hold'em poker game organised by one of Fleming's best villains, Le Chiffre. I learned Texas Hold'em, teaching myself via an app, and then played a lot online. Too much. I had to stop, not because I was losing – I was breaking even overall and anyway, I never played for high stakes – but because it is very addictive and time-wasting. No, not 'wasting'. I enjoyed it, it was a mental challenge, and I was improving all the time. But time-consuming, certainly. I began to find myself playing every night until the early hours. Time to stop. But knowing the game has made re-reading *Casino Royale* much more exciting. Gambling at the tables lends itself to great set-piece scenes in fiction. At the beginning of *Daniel Deronda*, George Eliot created a magnificent one in the casino at the fictional German spa town of Leubronn, based on the one at Baden-Baden. That casino is still where it was in her day, and unchanged other than having been given a fresh coat of paint and new upholstery and drapery, though always in the same white, gold and red. In Anthony Trollope's Palliser novel *Can you Forgive Her?*, the aristocratic wastrel Burgo Fitzgerald loses everything on the spin of the roulette wheel. Dostoevsky's *The Gambler* is a whole novel about good and evil forces played out in the casino.

Le Chiffre is a magnificent and entirely credible villian, which some of Fleming's are not, and if a villain is not credible, he can't frighten you, whereas Le Chiffre is terrifying.

So is Sir Hugo Drax, in *Moonraker*, which I rate as by far and away the best Bond, and the one which can take its place with a lot of good literature – the novels of Graham Greene, for a start. It has a more sombre theme than the other Bonds, one which becomes worryingly more relevant more or less every decade. Every time North Korea raises its head I am reminded of *Moonraker*.

If Ian Fleming wrote another gambling scene to rival the poker game Bond plays against Le Chiffre, it is the one in *Moonraker* in which he plays against Drax at bridge and uncovers his (fiendishly clever) habit of cheating. The game takes place at Blades, the archetypal St James's gambling club, where the food and wine are superb, the club servants impeccable, the surroundings elegant and hushed. The scene, in which the room, and its tables, gradually fill up, and the games commence, with a pall of cigar and cigarette smoke hanging under the shaded lamps, is one of Fleming's finest pieces of writing. I do not understand or know bridge, as I know poker, but I can just about follow what is going on and feel the mounting tension as Sir Hugo Drax gets bolder and bolder in his cheating and Bond closes in on him.

Moonraker began life as a screenplay, via which Ian Fleming hoped to make a fortune – and indeed he did make one, but out of the film of his next novel, not this one.

I don't like the Bond films much – the only exception is the 2006 version of *Casino Royale* starring Daniel Craig. Sony Pictures swapped the rights in James Bond with MGM – in exchange for those to *Spider-Man*. I would love to know which has made more money and if either regrets the deal.

———— ●○● ————

THIS BEING EXAMINATION MONTH, panic rolls over to my side of the fence. They are cramming at the last minute to answer GCSE questions on *The Woman in Black*. Most students are fine, and I can calm them down with a simple answer to a sensible question. And then there are the others. They haven't read the 'whole book' until now – dear God!

It isn't even long. They think that, because I wrote it, I know the right answers and will tell them, so that they can get A*s – never understanding that there are no 'right answers' in this sort of thing, as there are in maths or chemistry. It is about what their own reading of the text is, what it tells them, and whether they can demonstrate how they arrived there. The book stands alone. If they think a certain element 'means' something and can show why, then it does, even though I did not put the meaning there and may even disagree with it. This seems to be a near-impossible concept to explain. All they can see is that I am the one who wrote it, ergo I know.

They are not always well taught and come up with some difficult and half-baked theories. They also cannot quite grasp – and this does sound ridiculous – that these character *do not exist,* and so have no past or future outside of the book. I do try to help but I do not envy their teachers. I also rather mind when I spend a couple of hours answering a whole class's questions, via the teacher – only for my reply to vanish into the ether, followed by silence. I rarely get thanked.

Each time another round of these questions comes in, I vow not to reply. But it is not the fault of this year's lot that last year's lot had no manners. So I sigh and answer. And just occasionally along comes one who lets me know that she/he got their A*. 'It was all down to you, miss. You're a legend.' Nice to know.

———◆·○·◆———

'TREACHEROUS MONTH, MAY.' My father – a glass half-empty man if ever there was one. But it certainly can be, with wild gales and lashing rain beating down the best flowers. Apart from roses, everything I love most comes in May. Tree peonies. Iris. May blossom. And never mind that it is a 'weed', cow parsley. The line of Iris pallida (dalmatica), a breathtaking blue, is slowly increasing in the starved soil below the low wall. They like starvation. All the sweet-smelling shrubs start now. Philadelphus. Lilac. There is wild lilac along the lane to the ford and, as soon as that fades, the wild honeysuckle flowers take over. I learned the hard way that if you want the best smelling honeysuckle, you avoid anything from a nursery/garden centre, but find instead the wild sort, straggling over a wayside hedge, take a stem for cuttings and go that way. This has not had the scent bred out of it.

Bluebells come, usually the Spanish sort, but in woods everywhere they mesmerise with their sheets of blue – a blue like no other. No wonder it is said to be a healing colour. Look at a copse of bluebells long enough and you feel calm and serene and healed in spirit.

But this year, the rain and the gales have beaten everything in the garden into sad submission. There has been no point in putting out the tables and chairs. The skies are thunderous and scudding across above us. It is cold.

The next morning, when Thomasin withdrew the curtains of her bedroom window, there stood the Maypole in the middle of the greek, its top cutting into the sky. It had sprung up in the night, or rather early morning, like Jack's bean-stalk. She opened the casement to get a better view of the garlands and posies that adorned it. The sweet perfume of the flowers had already spread into the surrounding air, which, being free from every taint, conducted to her lips a full measure of the fragrance received from the spire of blossom in its midst. At the top of the pole were crossed hoops decked with small flowers; beneath these came a milk-white zone of Maybloom; then a zone of bluebells, then of cowslips, then of lilacs, then of ragged-robins, daffodils, and so on, till the lowest stage was reached. Thomasin noticed all these, and was delighted that the May revel was to be so near.

The Return of the Native, my introduction to Thomas Hardy at A Level, and the start of a life of admiration and pleasure. That passage is a little more lyrical than his usual. Hardy was a melancholic man, glass only a quarter full. He had no optimism, no hope for man or the universe. 'The President of the Immortals ... had finished his sport with Tess' is surely one of the bleakest sentences in English literature. *Tess of the d'Urbevilles* and *Jude the Obscure* – the only two I never got on with and cannot re-read. *The Return of the Native* is still my favourite, though the masterpiece is *The Mayor of Casterbridge*. What a delineator of character he was. And people talk about Jane Austen.

————•○•————

WALKED ALONG THE MARSHES at low tide. Oystercatchers and redshanks feeding in the mud. Then, dipping its beak in and skimming it along for a yard, lifting it, skimming again, there was a spoonbill. They were almost extinct in Britain and then they hung on and started to breed and spread and now, especially here, they are fairly common. Egrets were very rare in the early twentieth century; now I see them every time I go to the marshes.

I saw a spoonbill at Morston marshes recently, and that once unbelievably rare bird, the black-winged stilt. Not quite so rare now, though, since a pair bred on the Wash.

Sam West, the actor and passionate birder, says the rarest he has ever seen was a black-faced spoonbill, in Hong Kong. Apparently there are only 2700 of them in the world. How do they *know* that? Waders and shore birds belong in the Ministry of Funny Walks.

Is a sense of humour one of the things that sets the human race apart? Animals and birds do things that look funny to us but do they know what 'funny' is? Do they have/understand jokes? How can we know? Yet they play, and not only when young.

And not only with humans, who buy them squeaky toys and catnip mice. Poppy and Orlando, dog and cat, play together, aged ten and nine, chasing games, hide and seek through the long grass, 'biffing' games.

---●·◦·●---

Here comes the sun, here comes the sun,
And I say it's all right ...

READING IN THE GARDEN is a pleasure after being stuck inside through the long wet chilly days in which you feel summer is already slipping past. If you are a reader, you read anywhere. The children used to read walking along the street, and so bumped into things. Trains and boats and planes. Chair. A hammock. When we had a hammock, that was a great reading place but there are not the right trees here. The bath (but probably not the shower). Bed, of course. Which heroine was it who read curled up inside the Hons cupboard? Oddly, in spite of 'beach reads', I have never read on beaches because I don't lie out in the sun, my beaches are for walking on in winter. Sitting on the dock of the bay. Watching the tide roll away Watching children and dogs run about.

The parasol and white sand and hot sun and long cold drinks probably make for other sorts of reading, light fiction that doesn't touch the sides. Whoever saw anyone reading James Joyce or Dr Johnson on a beach?

⬤•O•⬤

PRIZES HAVING MEANT SO MUCH when I was a young writer, I was thrilled to win the Somerset Maugham Award in 1971, which gave me £500 to be spent on travel. How far would that get me now? Instead of going to Ulan Bator or across the Atlas mountains by yak, I took the night train to Venice and spent six weeks there on the money, staying in a tiny but pleasant and clean hotel and living on their breakfasts and then cheap fruit from the market and tiny pizzas. The orchestras in St Mark's Square were outrivalling each other with the theme from *Love Story* and, as I could never afford a coffee at Florian's, I just walked about, hearing them down every side alley. It was an extraordinary time and I wrote about Venice a great deal afterwards. And thanked Maugham from the heart, every day. A friend who had known him said he was 'a crocodile', and so he may have been – though he looks more like a very old tortoise in the marvellous Graham Sutherland portrait. I will not hear a word said against him. But I did not know his books when I won the award. My mother had been an avid reader of his. My university tutors turned up their noses, as indeed did almost everyone then.

'Such a tissue of clichés that one's wonder is finally aroused at the writer's ability to assemble so many and at his unfailing inability to put anything in an individual way' was a typical dismissal. Edmund Wilson who wrote that, had cloth ears. Maugham writes beautifully, as I discovered. His prose is cool and clear and elegant and he sums up a character, a place, a point of view, a relationship time and time again, in a perfect sentence.

I came across this:

As the sun was setting I wandered into the Mosque. I was quite alone. As I looked from one end along the chambers into which it is divided I had an eerie, mysterious sense of its emptiness and silence. I was a trifle scared. I can only put what I felt into words that make no sense. I seemed to hear the noiseless footfall of the infinite.

I suppose most people who have been alone in an ancient church or other place of worship have had that sensation. It is the same as going into a church after a funeral or a wedding or other service, after everyone has left, and feeling that the prayers and the music are somehow still there, being absorbed into the atmosphere, into the very fabric of the building, and yet also being available to the solitary visitor. Being by oneself in such places can be moving, or disturbing – but it is not usually at all frightening.

Maugham says that his words make no sense, but of course they do.

The quotation comes from his *A Writer's Notebook*, which he kept for much of his life and filled with observations, records of conversations, short descriptions, comments on being a writer. The edition I have is unsatisfactory in that everything is run together without divisions. The only separations are for the date at the beginning of each new year – it runs from 1892 to 1949. There should have been at the least some space between each entry – it is confusing to read and sometimes, as one reads one paragraph straight after another, it is nonsensical. Still, there is much richness in it and, after a few pages, I found that it was best just to dip in. Towards the end, he says things about growing older which I did not understand until I was seventy myself.

> *... it occurred to me that the greatest compensation of old age is its freedom of spirit.*
>
> *I suppose that is accompanied by a certain indifference to many of the things that men in their prime think important. Another compensation is that it liberates you from envy, hatred and malice. I do not believe that I envy anyone. I have made the most I could of such gifts as nature provided me with; I do not envy the greater gifts of others. I have had a great deal of success. I do not envy the success of others ... I no longer mind what people think of me. They can take me or leave me.*

(Mind you, I have met some writers who, even in old age, bitterly envy the success of others and are still ready to deride them.)

On the evidence of this book alone, Maugham was a reflective man, and he seems to have made his observations about human nature, writing, life, only after careful thought and the weighing of arguments. Perhaps this is an illusion. He may have jotted things down 'off the cuff', but it never seems so. He is worth reading for his balanced mind and judgement alone.

The game of 'best novel' is fun to play but not worth too much because, although literary experience and critical judgement play a part, in the last resort this is largely a matter of personal opinion. I have not read all of Maugham by any means, and some of his best-known books – *Liza of Lambeth, The Moon and Sixpence* – are not really to my taste. Given that I often find more in a short novel than a long one, it is not surprising that I so admire *The Painted Veil*, which is really a novella. It is a small masterpiece. There is not a word spare. Not a sentence overlong. Maugham was so good on women. He understood infidelity and the way some women of his time led pointless lives, through no fault of their own, the wives of those in the colonial service of the old days probably more than most. He understood boredom and lassitude and the effects of an extreme climate, to which the English were unaccustomed. He understood the formality of that society and how stifling as well as false it could be. And so he understands the heroine of this painful, vivid novel about a woman, Kitty Garstin, who marries her scientist husband Walter for no better reason than that her younger sister has announced her engagement and so is about to upstage her. They go to Hong Kong, where he works as a bacteriologist and Kitty, who does not love her husband, embarks on an affair with a charming and unreliable colonial civil servant, Charlie Townsend. Inevitably, the story ends tragically. The oppression of the climate, the stiff society, the landscape which seems so alien, the natives who are even more so, the unhappy marriage and the pull of the affair with the handsome 'bounder' Charlie – all of these catch and hold the reader from the beginning in a tense, claustrophobic atmosphere. It is a book that asks to be read in one intense sitting and we come out of it not quite knowing where we are.

WSM was a fine short-story teller, best perhaps when reigned in tightly. In his day, he was a successful and popular dramatist – at one time he had four plays running at the same time in London's West End. No wonder he made a great deal of money. He was generous, giving a lot of it away, during his lifetime and after his death, including a chunk to endow the prize for a writer under the age of thirty-five which was of so much value to me at just the right moment in my career. Crocodile or not, I salute him.

————•O•————

THE CUCKOO IS DRIVING ME MAD, from dawn, yet for several years he was barely heard here. I defy anyone to explain. The only time I saw, as against heard, one was when I went out to investigate a bird racket close to the house and saw a mass of swallows, house martins, blue tits and goodness knows what else mobbing a hapless cuckoo around the old walnut tree. There must have been twenty birds diving and bombing until they saw him off.

————•O•————

I WRITE IN MY BOOKS and I have done so ever since university, when one of the pleasures of buying text books from those going down was trying to decipher the margin notes and underlinings, going back through several previous owners. They were often useful, sometimes not. My university edition of F. N. Robinson' s *The Complete Works of Geoffrey Chaucer* is so littered with margin notes and underlinings that the text has a struggle to make itself heard. I still underline, scribble, fold down corners. I like to have a physical relationship with my books.

————•O•————

I AM GRADUALLY BUILDING UP my book pile for France again, in June this time. Taking the car means there is plenty of space. I have put *Moby Dick* first. And then taken it out again. Decided on *Our Mutual Friend*, for the annual Dickens. And changed it for *Little Dorrit*.

I ought to add something in French, so I put in a copy of *Le Petit Prince*, Antoine de Saint-Exupéry's beguiling story written in an elegant and straightforward French I can understand. The same applies to Georges Simenon's detective stories, but all my copies of the Maigret novels are in English so I will have to wait and buy one in Montcuq or Prayssac, both of which small market towns in the Lot have shops selling, as well as newspapers, magazines, stationery, maps, postcards, toys and sweets, a good range of books, new and classic titles, in hard and paperback. I am quite likely to find one or two Simenons in the local supermarket, as he is ever popular, never out of print.

I want to start a three- or four-volume series. Olivia Manning's war novels were last summer. In previous years, I have worked my way through Paul Scott's *Raj* and Lawrence Durrell's *Alexandria* quartets, and Evelyn Waugh's *Sword of Honour* trilogy.

Now I'm stuck. Twitter comes to my aid, as usual, in the shape of Patrick McGrath, who reminds me of Gormenghast among other things.

■•○•■

HOW MANY PEOPLE are there living in the books here? Only take the complete novels of Dickens and add up all the characters in each one and then multiply by … and I already need to lie down. Overall, there must be thousands of imaginary people sharing this house with us. Silent. Invisible. Dead? No, not dead, or at least not permanently. They spring to life when someone opens the book in which they are held prisoner ... But of course they don't. They do not spring to anything, least of all life. And yet they come alive in the mind, in the imagination of the reader. In one sense, anyway.

It is not quite the same with real people who once actually lived, and yet, in reading about them, the same process happens ... One reads about them on the page and they come alive in the imagination and the mind. In the case of those one has known in life it is in the memory. But they are still no longer flesh and blood and life and spirit, they are still just 'people in books', and we get to know them in exactly the same way as we do those fictional characters who never did exist. So literature is the great leveller.

In a sense.

This kind of thing keeps me awake at night.

———●•○•●———

HAY LIT FEST TIME. Hay-on-Wye, charming little town on a hill right on the Welsh borders. Good shops. A thousand bookshops. Llangoed Hall, the excellent hotel in the country a few miles away that used to belong to Laura Ashley's husband, Bernard Ashley. He arrived by helicopter onto the front lawn from his home across the valley in Wales.

I did gigs at Hay several times and great fun they were. The Hay Festival used to be sponsored by the *Guardian*, but it has run through quite a few supporters in its time. It vies with Cheltenham for attracting the Big Names, but Hay takes it one further in that they are not always Literary Names, they are bigger than that.

Bill Clinton lectured there and called it 'The Woodstock of the Mind'. That pleased them.

Talk of Hay leads back to Haymakers I have met, leads back to Christopher Hitchens and Susan Sontag and Martin Amis. Not sure where to start.

Martin, I think. Yes. Because he only has a walk-on role in this and he is blameless. I have known him since he was, I think, sixteen. I admire his early novels greatly. *London Fields*, *Money* ... He wrote like an angel then, and he still does, but the subject matter and characters of some of his later novels has not equalled the greatness of the prose. Well, that has happened to plenty of other writers and I will never give up on him. I am also very fond of him, though we rarely meet now because he lives in New York. We have a closer tie, too, and not only because I knew both his father Kingsley and his stepmother Elizabeth Jane Howard. Martin's cousin Lucy was murdered by Fred West. Lucy's mother was a friend – I knew her first when Lucy was still a 'missing person'. I did not know much about it, other than the snippets of information hurriedly imparted by mutual friends before I met her. And then the terrible truth emerged. It was unimaginably dreadful, the worst possible conclusion to twenty-odd years of not knowing. How does one look someone in the eye when they have experienced all of that? It is very, very hard. And there are absolutely no words. None at all.

But Martin managed words, as only he could. He wrote about Lucy in his memoir *Experience*, with such love, such joyful recollection of their childhood days, and such grief and pure, white-hot anger about her death. Reading it takes one through all of those emotions. It is cathartic but one of the few pieces of such writing which does not heal, because how can it? Words cannot heal or help such evil and suffering. I truly believe there is a limit to what even words can do and here one reaches it. My admiration for Martin the writer was always great, but after he wrote *Experience* it is respect that I feel most strongly, and that will never weaken.

At Hay, in May 2000, I was coming out of my room on the upper floor of the Llangoed at the same moment that Martin was emerging from his, opposite. We had an intense conversation on the landing, a catch-up, a sharing of distress about Lucy – we didn't talk about books apart from *Experience*. Our intermittent friendship has always come from a different place. We went down the rather grand staircase. He was meeting some friends for tea, and then they were all going over to do a gig at the festival.

The friends, who arrived as Martin and I parted, turned out to be Christopher Hitchens and Susan Sontag, sweeping into the large hotel lounge, he taking his coat off while keeping a cigarette in his mouth, she – well, just sweeping.

I was busy for the rest of that day and evening, but the next morning, waiting in the entrance for the taxi taking me to my own event in Hay, I was joined by Susan Sontag. She was a handsome woman – she had been extremely beautiful when younger – but also absolutely formidable, terrifyingly serious and very clever. The archetypal bluestocking. Self-aware. Self-important? Well, she was certainly conscious of her own status. I had read a lot of her essays and journalism and admired such of it as I fully under-stood – the references are often pretty obscure, especially those to art films and foreign literature, and the arguments are not always easy to follow. Wit is there, shafting through the uber-intelligent prose, but humour never. You get no jokes with Sontag and stand-ing in the spring sunshine with her that morning, waiting for our respective cars, I was aware that small talk and chit-chat would be quite inappropriate. But I muttered something about the beauty of the late May morning and, for a moment or two, in response, she opened out like a flower. She had been driven through the lanes to the hotel the previous afternoon and they had been thick with blossom, the trees that fresh, first yellow-green before the deadness of high summer thickens and dulls them. And, she said, 'I just felt I was being given such a privilege. Such a privilege to be in the midst of it all.'

It was such an unlikely sentiment for this serious intellectual woman to express and, for a moment, we agreed and smiled and then just stood, basking in such a day and what, I realised, was indeed a privilege.

And then, out of the doors behind us burst Hitchens, and Martin. Mart mentioned something about my having known Kingsley, and Hitchens said something sarcastic. 'No,' I said. 'Contrary to the impression he liked to give, Kingsley was very proud of Martin.' Susan Sontag said this put a new complexion on that particular father–son relationship, but she seemed doubtful. Hitchens continued to sneer as he strode off, cigarette, as ever, in the corner of his mouth. Their cars came, Mart gave me a quick hug, the others did not bother to say goodbye and they rolled off. My own cab appeared and we didn't meet again, because our events were in separate corners of the festival tent-city.

Both Sontag and Hitchens died within the next few years, both from horrible forms of cancer. Hitchens, whom I admired but could not like, met it head on with great and public bravery. Susan Sontag had already had two rounds in the ring with cancer and come out fighting. This time, she went down fighting, desperate and defeated and perhaps feeling the loss of dignity and powerful intellect as much as the pain.

I have been reading a book called *The Violet Hour* by Katie Roiphe, in which she gives accounts of some great writers during their last weeks and days, facing death. The chapter on Sontag is tough, because her sickness and her absolute desperation to go through anything, anything, to buy herself more life are terrible to read about. Long after most people would have given up, she was trying the cruellest of treatments which had scant chance of success. Doctors ought to be ashamed of themselves for giving out the infinitesimal morsel of hope along with these barbaric procedures. Stem cell replacement was the worst of all. It was clear to everyone around her that the treatment was not working and she was dying, hideously, painfully, but they none of them dared to suggest to her that she give up. She was not a woman you argued with. She had survived against the odds before. She believed she always would. Roiphe is tough on Sontag: 'From girlhood [her] private mythology was predicated on a contempt for the ordinary and a distance from it.'

Her son, David, 'was amazed by his mother's continuing faith in medicine and by her ability to beat the odds. At the worst moments, he thought to himself, She really does not know what is happening to her; she still believes that she is going to survive. It was part of his role, as he saw it, to mirror this belief back to her as best he could.'

It is beyond sad. To be unable to face death, to be defiant, to go through the worst of physical and mental pain, because of an inability even to contemplate the idea that there might be a spiritual dimension to life – and to death and after-death – because of an intellectual arrogance. How terrible must that be? Christopher Hitchens was the same, of course. The intellect, the mighty brain, the pride, the stubbornness – how they stand in the way of any gentleness or humility, let alone any kindness to the self. An open mind is surely best in the face of death, because intellectual pride and arrogance, and how your fellows, who hold the same position, think of you, gets you nowhere. Belief, admitting the possibility of another dimension, of a spiritual side to humanity, is no more of a sure thing than negativity, but at the very least it is a comfort – and what is wrong with that?

I have had too much personal evidence of the presence of the dead, too many clear hints of a glorious after-life, to ignore. I would not make these up to comfort myself but they are an inexpressible consolation in the face of death. Would I deny them in the face of the sneers and jeers of others? If I did, I would be untrue to myself and my own experiences. I respect the unbelief of others. They should respect my faith. None of us can prove anything either way, to the satisfaction of the others, this side of the grave and to dent that is another sort of arrogance.

I felt both sad and moved, reading about Susan Sontag's end. No human being should have to die like that. She never came to terms with her own mortality, which reveals her as fearful and fearfully human.

It is in this context that I will always remember those moments on the steps of the hotel, in the May sunshine, when she said that seeing the spring countryside had been 'such a privilege'.

Friday 3
Frost, ice, sun and clouds, clear.

Saturday 4
Dark & sharp.

Monday 6
Snow, sleet, cold, rain.

Wednesday 8
Frost, ice, sun and clouds, louring.

Thursday 9
Grey & mild. Dark & mild.

Friday 10
Sunny & hot, heavy clouds, bright & chill.

(The tortoise weighs 6lb 11 ounces
he weighed Spring 1781 6 lbs 8 ounces
May 1780 6lbs 4 ounces)

So notes Gilbert White. It is always a joy to read his *Natural History of Selborne*, at random, or 'on this date' 250 years ago … He seems so close to us, with his weather and nature and gardening reports. So many things remain. He waits for the first hirundines, records when the swifts are very late, weighs the tortoise and seems to grow enough cucumbers to feed the county. He feels friendly to me as I read, cheerful, methodical, modest, inquisitive, a man as in tune with the natural world around him as if it were part of him, and allied to the blood running through his own veins, his breathing and the movements of his limbs. He is lovable, as Kilvert is lovable. There is so much to love in these old country parsons. White is useful, too, for correcting one's feeling that never was a July as hot as this, swallow so early, oak so late in leaf, winter so mild, tortoise so regular in its habits. The sun rises and sets and the moon waxes and wanes and the tides are high and then low and the Earth turns on its axis, for us as for Gilbert White. That is comforting.

JUNE

THE MERRY-GO-ROUND of literary prizes starts here. First it was the Orange. Then the something or other and then the Baileys Women's Prize for Fiction and now the Women's Prize for Fiction – not as many new names as that big non-fiction award which has gone through so many changes of clothing. The Samuel Johnson Prize suited it very well but now it's the Baillie Gifford.

It ill behoves me to complain that there are too many book prizes, having won some in my early career. They came at just the right time, they were lifesavers in terms of the money, but more – they gave me confidence that I was right all along. They were recognition. And they are *there*. No one can take them away. Forty-five years later, they still count.

So I can't complain. But every year the prizes proliferate and every year, a few of them at least come to mean less – particularly the lucrative prizes for the best short story of the year. £20K or £30K for one story? These almost always go to unknowns who may have written a single stunning story and then vanish without trace. The point about book prizes is partly to give the recipient's career a boost, to provide time and financial support for them to climb the next rung of the ladder.

One writer who won a major prize a few years ago and whose book went on to be a bestseller said that she didn't think she would bother to write another. Up to her, of course, but it seemed churlish, like being given a gold medal for your first attempt at the long jump and saying you can't be bothered to continue in the sport.

People will always disagree about the winner of any of the big prizes. The howls of dismay and protest that sometimes greet the Best Show Garden at Chelsea are often loud. But that is not the same as seeing conspiracy theories, deriding the judges, or insisting that they had 'a hidden agenda'. Having been a judge for most of the major fiction prizes and twice for the Man Booker, I can say with a completely clear conscience that our panels had no hidden agendas – our only thought was the responsibility of choosing the best book. Not the best author. Not because it was 'Buggins' turn'. Not because we thought it should go to a woman. Or someone gay. Or black. Or transgender. Not because anything. During the last Man Booker Prize I judged, we had heated arguments, and the late Ion Trewin, most loved of bookmen, had almost to wade in and separate one or two of us. But when we had decided on the shortlist, we then asked him to tell us how many novels by women we had selected and to give us the break-down on which publishers had books on the shortlist. We genuinely had no idea about either because neither had been relevant.

There is a huge amount of money lavished on these things – not so much in terms of the winner's booty, but on judges' fees and publicity and PR companies and on the prize-giving dinner. Whether this is all worth it for the prize backers I have no idea. I cannot think that it is, but it's their money.

And if a first-timer wins a Big Prize – especially one that garners masses of publicity – a heavy, heavy burden is laid on them for the whole of their future career. 'Follow that!' It's the same with silly-money advances for beginners. A man wrote one promising, though not flawless, first novel a couple of years ago. The publisher threw a lot of money at its launch and promotion. It did OK – better than many a first novel. But not much more than OK. Now it is announced that they have given him a contract for his next book worth £400K. Now, we all know that £400K is not what it seems. Advances always unravel the next morning. They are divided into segments – so much on signature, on delivery and acceptance of the manuscript, on hardback publication, on paperback publication … less the author's agent's 15 per cent, less income tax, blah blah. But £400K is still way too much for a second novel. The weight of expectation on that writer's back is too heavy. Sure, he may live up to it. But he may not. And if 'not' is the case, his career is probably over. There is no such thing as a free lunch, not even in the book world.

A couple of years ago, eligibility for the Man Booker Prize was opened up to novelists from the USA, having previously been for those from the UK and Commonwealth only. It was a bad idea. The major sponsor wanted global exposure to their brand, which probably makes sense from their point of view but does not make any from that of writers and publishers here in the UK. In 2016 an American won the prize. Statistically, this is likely to keep happening and British and Commonwealth novelists will be pushed out. There is no American prize for which we are eligible. Julian Barnes has made this same point. I hate crying 'Unfair', but this is a case of 'If it ain't broke, don't fix it.' Though not for the piper who calls the tune.

LIT FESTS. Victoria Wood could have done a great sketch about them – the people who are in the paying audience, the authors, the organisers, the …

I have done my share and I rarely agree to speak at them now – though the one I did in Whitstable recently was a pleasure. What makes lit fests work well are attentive, interested audiences of people who actually buy books afterwards, highly efficient organisation, friendly helpers, everything to do with the tent or hall or room in which one speaks working properly and, if there is an interviewer, one who has done his/her homework and is adept at opening the discussion up, prompting the right comments, steering the speaker back to the topic in hand, not putting self forwards … It is an expert job. The first time I did it I learned a lot within the hour – mainly that, although the speaker relies on the interviewer, in their turn they rely on the speaker. It can be smooth sailing and it can be like wading through mud at low tide. Beryl Bainbridge was a breeze, and great fun to talk to. So was Debo Devonshire. A nameless novelist far too big for their boots and unwilling to engage with either me or the audience made me vow never to do this thing again.

At Whitstable, I found myself wondering how the smaller festivals survive. Large lit fests get large sponsorship, from newspapers or TV companies or local magnates with deep pockets and cultural aspirations. Small ones survive on volunteers and goodwill. Often they cannot pay authors, in which case the authors have to decide whether the gig is worth their while.

But the joy of the lit fest is meeting with people who come to say they have always loved your books, or that this one has meant much to them, or that one kicked off their teenager's love of reading, or was their late mother's favourite … not to mention the old school and university friends and former neighbours who pitch up. I asked the organiser of one small book festival why they didn't apply for Arts Council or area arts funding. They had. They were turned down because lit fests are, apparently, too middle class.

———•○•———

A COUPLE OF YEARS AGO I was asked to contribute a short story to an anthology, edited by Tracy Chevalier, commemorating Charlotte Brontë's anniversary, with the title, and theme of, *Reader, I Married Him*. I usually have no hope of writing a short story to a particular brief, or indeed, to commission at all. They don't come to order. But I had been reading every book I could find about Edward VIII – the Duke of Windsor, as he became – and Wallis Simpson, of which there are many. They and their story have continued to exert a fascination with the British public, even so many years after the events, and I realised that I could write a story loosely about not so much 'them' as 'her' on the theme.

Having read so much, and then written it, my mind of course went back to 5 June 1972 and the Duke's funeral.

Three months earlier, after David had died, I was in a bad way and I needed my friends, especially those who had been close to him, too. Stephen Verney, who was such a good support and friend to me when we were both connected with Coventry cathedral, and who was one of David's friends, as well as colleagues, had moved on to become a Canon Residentiary at St George's Chapel, Windsor. He and his wife Scilla asked me to go and stay with them there, at 4 The Cloisters, when I liked, for as long as I liked. The visit was life-saving for me.

It also happened to be at the time of the death of the Duke of

Windsor. His funeral was in St George's Chapel, preceded by the lying in state of the former king, and of course Stephen was very involved in all of it.

On the first evening of the lying in state, he came to the drawing room, where I was with Scilla and one of their daughters, Rachel, playing some music – Rachel on the piano, me on the oboe. He said that if we could be almost invisible, and more silent than mice, but wanted to take part in a small bit of history, we should follow him.

We went in awe, and indeed in silence, to where he told us to conceal ourselves behind a stone pillar in the shadows, and to wait and watch. I remember it so well. I remember the extraordinary sense of that historic building all round us, and of the centuries and the events it had seen and the cold and weight of the very stones and the deep dimness. I remember being not entirely sure what we were there waiting for. And hardly daring to breathe. We all peered into a patch of grey light, beyond the shadows and the pillars, and, after a few moments, into that light a black car glided to a stop. Men in suits leaped out, looking around them, as the royal detectives do. We froze. Out got the young Prince of Wales and then, on the other side, our side, slowly, cautiously, stepped the Duchess of Windsor. Prince Charles went to her. She turned for a second and I can see vividly now the ashen pale face beneath a black hat and behind a black veil. I remember her stricken look, her face of grief and a sort of bewilderment, but a bearing of great dignity. And so they moved off towards the entrance to the chapel, where she would pay her last respects to Edward, the husband who had abdicated the throne for her, and had loved her, through all those years of dull, dreary exile.

It was history. I felt it as I have never felt it before or since – and how would I? Nobody else was there. Certainly no one knew that we were there, except Stephen. We waited, and eventually, very moved and thoughtful, crept back through the shadows again to the house, in even deeper silence and awe, and a sort of disbelief.

The next morning, I went with the Windsor household to process past the coffin in St George's Chapel. There he was. There were the soldiers standing guard. The tall candles flickering. The white flowers. The draped flag. The absolute stillness and silence, save for the slight sound of footsteps, soft on stone. The occasional muffled cough. As we went slowly past, the guard changed. The soldiers came to attention. Changed arms. Marched off, to be replaced by the next men. But their footsteps rang on the stone floor.

And then we went out into the June sunshine.

On the day of the funeral, we watched from the windows. Ted Heath, then Prime Minister, came to lunch – he and Stephen were old Oxford contemporaries and friends. What a bloodless, stuffy man he was – though perfectly pleasant and polite, and delighted with the curry Scilla had cooked. He loved curry, he said, 'and I very rarely get it', as if he could only ever eat what was put in front of him and had no say in the matter. Perhaps that was so.

That evening, I went into Stephen's study to fetch something for him and found his copy of the Order of Service for the funeral dumped in the waste paper basket. I stole it.

I have it here. I have slipped it into my copy of Philip Ziegler's biography of King Edward VIII. It is plain and simple, my small bit of English history.

And what of Wallis? Having read so much about her that I feel I know her better than she knew herself, I am still uncertain what to make of her – or indeed, of the whole story. It seems so complicated, but perhaps it isn't really. I don't think she ever meant him to abdicate for her. I think she would have been happy to be the royal mistress for however many years … After all, her first husband connived at the affair and indeed was rather proud of having a wife who was the King's mistress. It could have carried on more easily then than now. The media had not yet become all-seeing, all-knowing. Many of the country's citizens had no idea at all of what the King was up to, though the Court knew, Society knew. The former disapproved but the latter probably didn't care.

But his mother, Queen Mary, cared. And David Windsor, the King, cared, cared above all about having the throne with Wallis beside him as Queen. That he could never have. I don't honestly think it was what Wallis wanted. It all got out of hand and, before she knew it, she found herself divorced, exiled, not an HM or even an HRH, but merely the Duchess of Windsor, out of Society, out of favour, out of everything except his absolute slavish devotion and adoration. She married him.

What a tragedy it was. What a silly, weak, vain, ineffectual man he was. And what a load he dumped on his shy, stammering, unprepared brother, who only wanted to continue to be happily married and a loving father to his two daughters. Instead, he got lumbered with the throne and all the stress and distress that brought.

But of course if he had not been King, we would not have had Queen Elizabeth II – and what a splendid fist she has made of it, for longer than any other British monarch.

I put my Order of Service and the biography of King Edward VIII – David, Duke of Windsor – back on the shelf.

——■•○•■——

I SEE FROM MY LITERARY DIARY that today (22 June) was the birthday of H. Rider Haggard. Graham Greene always mentioned him as a formative influence – as a boy he was addicted to Haggard's adventure novels set in exotic places. The best known is *She* but Greene also loved *Allan Quartermain* and *King Solomon's Mines*. Greene wrote of Haggard: 'Enchantment is just what this writer exercised; he fixed pictures in our minds that thirty years have been unable to wear away.'

I tried to read them years ago, but gave up. They are boys' books really, though probably not for boys today. As a devoted reader of John Buchan's adventure novels, also sometimes set in far-flung parts of the old globe, I had expected to enjoy Rider Haggard. Never mind. Not everything lasts or goes around again and I doubt if he will.

Haggard was a Norfolk man and is buried in Ditchingham. It is the writings of his daughter, Lilias, that have helped me settle into this part of the world. She wrote for our local paper, the *Eastern Daily Press* – EDP – for years and they sometimes reprint her articles. I have her *A Norfolk Notebook* on my bedside table. It is now out of print but second-hand copies are easy to find round here. She knew North Norfolk as well as anyone ever has – its fields, lanes, marshes, villages, churches, coast. She sailed off Blakeney. She picked cockles at Morston and she saw many a rare bird at Stiffkey. Reading it, one feels that nothing changes. Lilias goes to a summer fete in one of those 'small agricultural villages which struggle so hard to save and support the heritage bequeathed to them by past generations – an ancient and lovely church'. I went to just such a fete last Saturday. The teas, the homemade cakes, the tombola, the ancient skittles, the whack-a-rat game, the jams and preserves, the book stall – all were in their usual places on the playing field ('if wet in Village Hall'). Those magnificent churches are still there, still needing support, and now with just a single vicar for four or five of them and services sometimes only one Sunday a month. But people still care for and about them very much. Only the second-homers are conspicuous by their absence from these occasions, as they are from the working parties to clean said church, or to paint the hall, or pick litter from the church environs. As ever, these jobs fall to the faithful few, some of whom try to relinquish the role of treasurer or clerk, but can never do so because no one will replace them. It was the same story when I lived in the Cotswolds. It is the same story throughout rural England.

At the top of the lane near to my house is a sign: 'To the Shell Museum'. It was a couple of years before I followed the sign, which led me to Glandford – through which the river runs, with a ford across it, like the one in this village. 'Unsuitable for Motors', the signs read, but so many people do not notice them or just ignore them and plough on, sinking as they go, and end up with sumps splitting on the rocky bottom and spilling oil down the river and, for them, an expensive call-out from the AA. Not far from the ford at Glandford is the Shell Museum, open from March to October. Let Lilias Rider Haggard describe it:

> *Thousands of shells from every part of the world are set out in all the glory of a myriad shades of pink and purple, green, orange, yellow, and a shimmering iridescence which has defied the years, locked away from the salt water in which they were born.*
>
> *They are mysterious things, shells, holding every colour of the sea*

and sky fixed and eternal, just as within them sings everlastingly the murmur of a ghostly tide. One wanders round, wondering which are the most beautiful. The big cowries blazing with the reds and oranges of the sunset. The mottled browns and purples of the 'plovers' eggs', which have a glaze unequalled in any china made by man. The thin, pearly substance of the fairy-like nautilus, who spread their frail sails to catch the wind on warmer seas than ours. Or the tiny, delicate shells which look as translucent as soap bubbles, frozen into immobility.

You can still see them, as she saw them. There is a modest entrance fee.

Nothing changes.

It was in *A Norfolk Notebook* that at last I found the prayer I had half-known for many years, but not who wrote it or its exact words. It was by Charlotte Mew – long-forgotten – though whether she actually wrote it herself or only took it down from someone else, I do not know. It is called 'The Old Shepherd's Prayer'.

Heavenly Master, I wud like to wake to they same green places
Where I be know'd for breakin' dogs and follerin' sheep.
And if I may not walk in th'old ways and look on th'old faces
I wud sooner sleep.

———◆•○•◆———

EVERY YEAR WE GO TO FRANCE for a month, either June or September, and if it is June, we therefore miss the irises, the best roses, the peonies … and the longest day, on which my lugubrious father always said, with gloomy satisfaction, that the nights had now started drawing in. But June is the best month in France. Their roses are in full spate, the swifts are in full flight, swooping and soaring and diving in and out of the church towers and the old barns.

Wild boar are menacing then, though, because they have young. We once smashed into a huge male as it ran straight across a long straight empty country road from the woods alongside. We hit it smack on and, as I caught a glimpse of its massive tusks and stiff bristle whiskers, I knew it was actually the Gruffalo. The thump as it hit the front of my 4 × 4 was frightening. I looked back and the boar was stone dead in the middle of the road and I knew I should have returned and … well, and what? An English friend who has lived in France for many years says he would have stopped, loaded it on to the roof rack and taken it home to cut up, cook and eat. 'Dinners for weeks, one way or another.' I ate wild boar once, in Germany. Have you ever chewed your own handbag, covered in red wine sauce?

———◆•○•◆———

A COUPLE OF MONTHS AGO I did a stupid thing in the heat of the moment. Who has not? It comes of impatience and impulsivity, which are slaves to modern technology. One used to be admonished to write a letter, out of anger and resentment or self-justification, in response to something hurtful or annoying and then either sleep on it before posting – or not posting – or tear it up immediately. Then along came email and the social media. If you are lucky, you can delete a post on Facebook or Twitter, but you cannot unsend or retrieve an email.

So, annoyed at something I read about a bookshop where I was to give a talk, I put up an angry post in response on Facebook. An editor read it and asked me to tidy it up and send it to the online edition of her magazine. From there it was picked up by the social and traditional media, and all hell broke loose. Well, I can deal with all hell. I have faced it often enough in my writing past. But for nine-tenths of that past the internet did not exist. Now it does and, in response to my article, as it had now become, Twitter broke loose and the ugly face of Twitter is not only not pretty, it is unutterably vile. Trolls, as they are called, patrol tweets, as they do newspaper articles online, prepared not only to jump into an argument – that would be fine – but to be abusive, threatening, vile, filthy-tongued and generally hurtful. I copped the full might of a Twitter storm, Force Ten, and the very moment it hit me I ducked out of the site altogether and did not read, reply to or comment on anything whatsoever for at least three weeks. It was more or less safe to go back after that.

But even the little I read, even the rest which friends and the not-so-friendly reported to me, made me understand how devastating being 'monstered' can be – not least because few people actually read and understand what you said originally and why you said it. They read what they think is there – no, *want* to be there. What it was all about was a nine-day wonder and there is no point in giving the thing further oxygen, but the effect was not simply bruising and annoying. I was accused, in disgusting language, of many things I was not in a million years guilty of – a fascist and a lackey of Donald Trump being the least of it.

I have been in the book world since 1960 and I have become, or so I thought, as tough as any. I do not flinch from a bad review so long as it is not personal – does not make unpleasant jibes at me, not my book – and does not show off at my expense. It helps if the reviewer has read the book attentively, too. I have dished out adverse criticism when reviewing, so I should be able to take it when it comes around to me. My lovely friend, the *Daily Mail* journalist Lynda Lee-Potter always answered her own phone if she was in the office – she said that if she dealt it out she ought to be able to take it.

Three months later and I am mended. Apart from one thing. The vileness thrown at me did not make me cry or even make me rage and storm. But it did, for the first time in fifty-seven years, cause me to lose my confidence as a writer. I simply could not write, or address any of the ideas that came to me, as they do, every day. I could not continue with the book I was planning. I could not think of myself as a writer any more.

And that was a first. I may not be many things, but I am a writer. It defines me. I have been one since the age of five and I have never been anything else – except for wife and mother and grandmother, but one's personal life is different.

So, there I was. A doctor friend of mine, a GP, was tricked and betrayed by her fellow partners, maligned and undermined by a process of passive-aggressive bullying, to the extent that she was forced to resign and lost her confidence as a doctor. She has not practised since – she took early retirement. It broke her, and when she was exonerated and proven innocent of all the trumped-up charges, it was too late. The damage was done. I would not claim that my case was remotely as serious as hers and, in any case, she was not to blame. Mine was self-inflicted. She cannot simply resume her professional life. A writer can. I have.

Then something else happened. While looking for something

– which I did not find – on the internet, I found instead a vicious article by a commentator not well known for his tact and sensitivity, about the novelist Rachel Cusk. I had not, at that stage, read any of her books, for no reason other than that one cannot read everyone. I then followed the trail and uncovered a whole library of antagonism, unpleasantness and worse about a book Cusk had written – not a novel but an account of her marriage breakdown. I did not go far before I then found an interview with her in which she confessed that, following the publication of this book and the subsequent public storm it had aroused, she was frozen, unable to write a new novel or even to think about one. I knew precisely what had happened to her because I had been in the same situation more recently, but in my case the freeze only lasted a month or two. Rachel Cusk was unable to write for *four years.*

I could do very little other than feel silent sympathy, except for one thing. It does nothing to make up for what happened to either of us, but writers are survivors and the one thing that keeps us going is the hope that people will buy and read and get something from our books. So I bought every Rachel Cusk book in print. They are stacked beside my bed, with the one about her marriage that roused the rabble at the top. Because honest, considered criticism and comment should be welcomed by all of us, but vile abuse and personal hostility and malevolent sneering from any commentator, public or private, should never be.

JULY

EBOOK SALES ARE DECLINING, but not before they have done permanent damage to one thing – not the physical, printed book, which is apparently thriving in both hard and paperback form, but the second-hand aka antiquarian book market.

I bought a book from a dealer last week which was not of great value per se but was out of print and needed by me – it was in fair condition and I might easily have chanced upon it in a charity shop for £1 but, of course, I might not – so I paid £12 for it. Plus postage. The dealer may well have got it from said charity shop himself. But it is all a game of chance and that book could well have been sitting on his shelves for five years.

A friend asked a second-hand book dealer to come and assess half of his book collection – some 2,000 volumes – to see what they might be worth and if he wanted them. The dealer offered £500. If that had been me, I would have refused, knowing that about twenty of the books alone were worth that and, having extracted said twenty and a few more, and having decided to keep, say, another couple of dozen, would have given the rest to an Oxfam bookshop. Instead, the friend decided to accept the £500, on the grounds that the man would take the books away and so he would be spared a lot of trouble.

It is not so long ago that second-hand book dealers could rip the public off and make a very handsome living for themselves. Not many people, unless they are specialists or in the trade, know the value of some of the books they own. Everyone thinks a signed copy of any Harry Potter book is worth a fortune, but I know someone who gave away three first editions of James Bond books to a charity shop and discovered that they had been worth around £30,000. He had bought them at the time they were published and kept them because he had the space. The charity shop got in touch with him when they found out how much the books were worth and asked my friend if he wanted to take them back, which was good and honest of them. He swallowed hard and said, 'No', which was good of him.

It must be difficult to scratch a living in the everyday second-hand book market. Occasionally I go into a dusty little shop and find so many easily obtained titles which are so grossly over-priced that I wonder who will ever buy them, when all people have to do is trawl through eBay to find what they want for a tenth of the amount. And there we have it. The internet has done the damage. Obviously, the really valuable rare book will always command a high price, but you are unlikely to find a twelfth-century illuminated manuscript or a Shakespeare first folio on eBay – that is another world – and if you only want to read the text of an out-of-print book, then so long as it is also out of copyright you are likely to find it, in full, on Project Gutenberg or some other free internet site.

I cannot help thinking that this is a good thing. It is a tricky area in which to set foot, this one of copyright, but I think that copyright should last for the lifetime of the writer plus ten years and no more. Why should not only an author's children but their grand- and great-grandchildren be able to live off the proceeds of their relative's hard work for their entire lifetimes? Because if an author has been famous and bestselling and continued to write and publish into their nineties, say, then that is what will happen, because at the time of writing copyright extends until seventy years after the death of the author. And that is not right. I wish there were some way of ensuring that my own books go into the public domain no more than ten years after my death.

———●○●———

IT ISN'T THE PLOT. It isn't even the characters – although they are some of the best ever created by a novelist. It is the writing. The style. And even more, the crisp one-liners, the short, dazzling paragraphs that make you trip over yourself. You might be forgiven for thinking that his books, like Shakespeare's plays, consist entirely of quotations:

She gave me a smile I could feel in my hip pocket.

From 30 feet away she looked like a lot of class. From 10 feet away she looked like something made up to be seen from 30 feet away.

Neither of the two people in the room paid any attention to the way I came in, although only one of them was dead.

It got dark and the rain-clouded lights of the stores were soaked up by the black street.

It was a blonde. A blonde to make a bishop kick a hole in a stained-glass window.

So Raymond Chandler does consist entirely of quotations, any one of which would make another writer proud to have composed.

He is in a class of his own, a genius pure and simple, and every single time I re-read *The Big Sleep*, or *The Little Sister*, or *The High Window* – any of them – I am struck by his genius, his wit, his command of the language. He makes it do exactly what he wants it to do, no less and no more, and that is a talent given to very few. He invented the mean streets, the hard-boiled private eye, the sleazy little hotels, the cocktail bars as seen by the cold light of day as well as by the neon light of 2 a.m. He owned the whole set-up and, although he has had imitators – not too many, because most wannabes back off the moment they have tried to construct a sentence like any of his – he brushed them off like specks of fluff on his sleeve.

As well as the brilliant novels, he wrote some of the best analysis of crime fiction, of what works, what does not, and any aspiring writer in the genre should read and take permanent note of his golden advice. And then, if he likes, ignore it. Chandler would have said that. There are no rules but there are plenty of sensible observations. The one I took to heart at the very beginning of writing a crime series was that no fictional private eye, or detective, should ever marry.

I have just found another quotation, which isn't a wise crack or a slick observation, just a piece of perfect descriptive writing (from *The High Window*):

The bar entrance was to the left. It was dusky and quiet and a bartender moved moth-like against the faint glitter of piled glassware. A tall handsome blonde, in a dress that looked like sea-water sifted over with gold dust, came out of the Ladies' Room touching up her lips, and turned towards the arch, humming.

I press Chandler on anyone who has not yet discovered him for themselves – and urge them to watch Humphrey Bogart as Philip Marlowe in any of the films. I have never had anyone tell me that either Chandler himself, or Bogart, failed for them.

I have often found people who failed with P. G. Wodehouse, though – another master of the language, another whose plots and characters are of second and third importance to the writing. But some cannot get past the receding chins, the brainlessness, the vacuousness, the frippery, the juvenile mentality of the characters. The only one to whom none of the above descriptions apply is, of course, Jeeves. Lord Emsworth sometimes succeeds where Bertie Wooster fails, but I never press home my argument about Wodehouse, because if the magic doesn't work, it doesn't and it never will. It is the uncomprehending reader's loss. Nobody half-likes Wodehouse (though the golfing stories fail with me because golf is of no interest and I don't understand the rules). You are an addict or you are left stone cold.

I have reminded myself to get *The Mating Season, Summer Lightning, Joy in the Morning, Right Ho, Jeeves, Lord Emsworth and Others* and others down from the long row of Everyman Wodehouse, in perfectly formed hardbacks, on the shelf in the lobby. A Chandler binge, followed by a PGW binge. If the weather holds, I can read them in a deckchair in the garden, which is where Lord Emsworth's brother Galahad Threepwood is generally to be found, a large whisky and soda to hand.

————■•O•■————

THE DEADLY MONTHS, July and August. The weather often disappoints, the birds have stopped singing, the roads round here are crammed with mobile homes and caravans being towed, the beaches are also crammed full and, yes, it is thoroughly selfish of me to complain about it. But winter is best here. Empty everywhere. In high summer it is best to get back from any shopping trip by ten o'clock and then stay in the garden, to read, or write, cold drink to hand, intermittently watching the swallows high overhead.

———•O•———

THERE ARE WATER VOLES nesting in the bank, just below the bridge over the ford. Children – and sometimes adults – play Pooh Sticks there, but the voles take no notice. Reminds me of Ratty in … actually not *The Wind in the Willows*, but the play by A. A. Milne, *Toad of Toad Hall*. It is still the best adaptation and the music crowns all. I have seen it so many times, including the 1970s RSC production in Stratford when Judi Dench was a very pregnant Mama Rabbit and Michael Williams, her husband, was Mole and Jeffrey Dench, her brother, played a very agile Ratty. I have often re-cast it in my mind and planned, if I win the lottery, to put it on for a run one Christmas. Stephen Fry would be Badger, David Walliams Toad, David Tennant Ratty. I have not yet found my perfect Mole.

There would, of course, be a proper orchestra, with a good conductor. I would ask Nicholas Daniel, who is up for anything.

Alan Bennett took over at one time, with his *The Wind in the Willows* for the National, but it was nowhere near as good as the Milne. Though, come to think of it, AB made a decent fist of Mole himself.

THE BIBLE IS WONDERFUL to read, no matter what one's personal belief. I would not be without the majestic language of the King James's Version, and Genesis, the Book of Job and Ecclesiastes and the Psalms, as well as the Gospels, which repay many a reading.

We do not often get the long-familiar words of the *BCP* funeral service now and Heaven help us looking to find one of the old hymns at a crematorium – though we may be luckier at church weddings. I hope they do not wither and fade like the flower and the grass. It is still possible to hear all the Songs of Praise well sung by choirs in recordings online and via CDs, though. Great to sing along to when travelling on a boring journey.

I sound like one of those people who lament that things have all changed and gone to the bad and everything new is by definition worthless, but I don't feel like that at all. Only the admonition not to throw the baby out with the bathwater is one to take seriously.

That the Bible and the Prayer Book can be sustaining is evident. Many people in dreadful circumstances have been strengthened, uplifted and given the hope and help to see them through by reading both. Not long ago, I learned that a priest I knew and admired greatly, the former Bishop of Gloucester, Michael Perham, was terminally ill with a brain tumour. He was a man whose books had impressed me with their clarity, faith and commitment to the Christian liturgy and I have read several of them often. He had sent out a last message to his former clergy, parishioners and friends, just before Easter this year, in which he explained that he was weakening but always sustained by his belief that he was being held in God's hands and upheld by those many who were praying for him – the 'Communion of Saints'. He ended by quoting a Collect and giving a blessing to us all.

(Bishop Michael died after having spent the Festival with his close and loving family on Easter Monday, 17 April 2017.)

I was reminded of Joseph Poole, friend, mentor and Precentor of Coventry Cathedral when I was part of that community, and who was one of the great liturgists of the Church of England. Also of Michael Mayne, former Dean of Westminster and one whose books have inspired and enlightened and sustained so many. All three men of faith and goodness have had an impact far beyond what may have been their own expectations, and that impact will continue to impact upon others.

Bishop Michael's last letter includes this, the Collect for All Saints Day from *The Book of Common Prayer*.

Almighty God
you have knit together your elect
in one communion and fellowship
in the mystical body of your Son Christ our Lord:
grant us grace so to follow your blessed saints
in all virtuous and godly living,
that we may come to those inexpressible joys
That you have prepared for those who truly love you;
through Jesus Christ your Son our Lord
who is alive and reigns with you
in the unity of the Holy Spirit
one God, now and for ever.

I often think that everyone has a lesson to teach, and it doesn't matter really what, so long as they do, and we learn it. Michael Perham was one who, like many others I have been blessed to

know, taught, among other things, how to die well. No matter
what faith the teacher has, or if they have none, no matter how
the lesson is taught, I wonder if there can be a more important
one. The test, of course, is if we have learned it well. And we won't
know that until our own time comes.

———————●•○•●———————

THE SPARROWS HAVE BEEN FLEDGING. There seem to be dozens
of nests, in the eaves, under the roof tiles, in the hedges all round
the village. When it rains, they are fluttering in the puddles, washing
themselves, I suppose, and, if it's dry, they are having dust baths. In
his *Natural History of Selborne*, Gilbert White records not only
dozens upon dozens of sparrows but of every other sort of 'common'
bird – thrushes, blackbirds, finches, tits – as well as the migrants …
flycatchers were everywhere. 'Are not two sparrows sold for a far-
thing?' Even in my own childhood, there were probably several
hundred per cent more song birds than now. The telephone wires
were lined with swallows and martins, the air thick with swifts.

The loss of so many over the last hundred or so years is forgotten – everyone talks about the pandas and the tigers and the
giraffes, and of course they are important. Meanwhile, not far
from home, people trap thousands of small birds for food. We are
reaping the whirlwind. I do not fuss greatly about climate change
because man does infinitely more harm in far more ways. But it is
distressing when people say they haven't heard a cuckoo for years
and yet that was a sound of my childhood that even became tire-
some, it went on so, from dawn to dusk through the spring and
early summer. Neighbours in this village say that twenty years ago
the house martins' nests lined the eaves the whole way round this

house. Now there are just three and last year they came late and barely managed a single brood.*

'Things are not what they were in my day.' Maddening how old people say it. But in this respect, and many others, I know it to be true. And 'things' have not been replaced by 'better things' either.

The sparrows are chatter-chattering in and out of the roof tiles as I write.

———•○•———

JOHN UPDIKE IS QUOTED AS SAYING of Muriel Spark that her novels 'remain in the mind as brilliant shards'. Is that how I would want to be remembered, as just a brilliant shard in someone's mind?

———•○•———

IT IS A SAD THING when you discover that a book you loved beyond many, a book of which you knew whole paragraphs and conversational exchanges by heart, a book you thought you would be wedded to for life, has lost its appeal, its charm, its ability to amuse and entertain, delight and impress. How does this happen? Does it mean the book has become dated, or outdated, its humour old-fashioned, its charm rusty, its brilliance tarnished? Was it a book you simply grew out of? Or one that, as you read more and got more life experience, could not keep up with you? Was it simply not up to the job, did it not bear any more re-readings, yield any more wisdom, reveal any new aspect to the wit, so that you laughed again but in a slightly different way?

---

* Summer 2017 – six nests.

What I am saying is that my love affair with E. F. Benson's Mapp and Lucia novels seems to be over. There are odd things that still delight: Quaint Irene, Georgie Pilson and his bibelots – a warm-hearted but wickedly funny camp character – the morning procession of women shopping in Tilling High Street while keeping beady eyes on what everyone else is doing, wearing, buying, saying. But I droop after reading three chapters of any of them and I no longer smile at all. It was a blow when this first happened. I decided it was just me and left the books alone for a while. But it went on happening. I found myself becoming impatient with these silly people – and that was fatal.

I don't expect to enjoy most children's books in the old way, though I have never wavered about the Moomin tales, or Alice, and I was very surprised to find I delighted almost as much when reading *The Magic Faraway Tree* to grand-daughter Lila as I did when I too was five years old.

But if ever Nancy Mitford or Dickens or Thomas Hardy fail me, I shall know my reading days are numbered.

WATCHED A HEN HARRIER on the marshes. There are several pairs, almost always visible, swooping across, looking for prey. They were rare once, but now they are common. The campaign to make hawks protected birds has seen to this, so they breed safely and murder small birds unhampered.

THE ONLY BOOK BY SHIRLEY HAZZARD I had read until recently was her memoir of Graham Greene, *Greene on Capri*. When

Hazzard died in December 2016 I took it down from the shelf, and also bought two of her novels and a book of essays. My passion for Graham Greene was probably at its height forty years ago, but the admiration has always been there, burning bright. Every time I have looked along the shelf where a dozen or more of his books sit and I have taken one down at random and read a few paragraphs, I have been reminded how great a writer he is.

Shirley Hazzard was married to the biographer Francis Steegmuller, and during the 1960s and 1970s, when Greene was in old age, they got to know him, and his last partner, Yvonne Cloetta, when they all spent weeks, sometimes months, on the island of Capri. They were friends, they went on expeditions together, met for drinks and lunches and dinners from time to time, talked endlessly, liked one another. Hazzard is so sharp about GG. She quickly recognised certain familiar traits in him, certain patterns of behaviour, anticipated them, watched them recur. She was both admiring and fond of him, but she was clear-eyed about his failings and flaws – not literary at all, but personal ones. He liked to throw a small bomb into the conversation and watch it explode. He liked to disagree, to argue, to fall out. He bore small grudges for a disproportionately long time. He was set in his ways, in Capri – 350 words, no more, no less, each morning, the same bar for drinks, the same café for dinner. A strange gap in his sensitivities was his lack of response to visual beauty, natural, architectural, pictorial. Nor was he at all interested in music. 'He almost never spoke to us of a painting or a painter, a piece of music or a composer … To have suggested that he visit a museum, attend an exhibition or a concert, was unthinkable.'

Literature was all to him, 'the longest and most consistent

pleasure of Graham's life'. Hazzard quotes Greene: 'One's life is more formed, I sometimes think, by books than by human beings: it is out of books that one learns about love and pain at second hand.'

In *Greene on Capri* I re-discovered a small masterpiece of biography, the story of a man caught and held in a particular period of his life, in just one place, which is both background, foreground and character. And in writing about the writer on the island, Hazzard also – almost inadvertently, perhaps – presents us with a quiet portrait of her own marriage to Steegmuller: contented, perfectly balanced, mutually responsive. By then, after a lifetime of intense, anguished loves, Greene himself was settled calmly, with the pert, pretty, slight, slim Yvonne, a woman with monkey looks, very short white hair, and an adoration of Graham which lasted over thirty years and was in such contrast to all his other tense, stressful, high-octane relationships. He was not a lover of women in general. He did not really rate them intellectually or spiritually. He was a man's man who fell in thrall to individual women, and lastly to Yvonne. Shirley Hazzard is critical, in a stern but understanding way, of his misogyny.

In John le Carré's interesting if enigmatic book *The Pigeon Tunnel: Stories from My Life*, Graham Greene is confirmed not only as a writer of spy stories but as a spy, working for MI6, but he pricks Greene's balloon of secrecy and self-importance neatly, in telling the story of the moment when at last GG was able to demand sight of his own FBI file. He had been convinced that he had been on the FBI blacklist of subversive pro-communists, but when he saw it he learned that, far from being so important that his file was a foot thick, in fact it contained only one entry – accusing

him of having kept company with the 'politically erratic' ballerina
Margot Fonteyn when she was fighting the (doomed) cause of her
Panamanian husband, Roberto Arias. But if Greene was a minnow
in the real world of spying, he caught its grubby and shadowy half-
life brilliantly in his fiction. Not, though, as brilliantly as le Carré
himself.

Having finished *Greene on Capri* again, I set about catching up
on Shirley Hazzard's other work, though it was in that book that I
first discovered her genius for the exact, perfect phrase. Describing
the Dottoressa Moor, an impossible Capri personality, she writes:
'A squat, categorical figure, formless in winter bundling, [she] had
the rugged, russet complexion of northerners long weathered in
the hot south … prominent paleolithic teeth, and memorably pale
blue eyes.' How much more clearly could we be made to see her?
And the paleolithic teeth …

Towards the end of the book, Hazzard recalls a visit of the man
who knew absolutely everybody, and about whom absolutely everyone seems to have written – Harold Acton. Describing Acton's
legendary good manners, she recalls someone saying that 'he was
a man who had never in his life preceded anyone out of a room'.

———◦———

ONCE UPON A TIME I had two shelves of books about Antarctica and
Antarctic exploration. I read them often, in love with those white
wastes, the last truly undiscovered, uninhabited places. Men like
Ernest Shackleton and Apsley Cherry-Garrard and Robert Scott and
their companions had ventured there, sometimes died there, facing
those desperate conditions of cold and white-out and disorientation
and a challenge that was as much emotional and psychological as

physical, but between them all they left very small tracks on those great white spaces, and those tracks were soon covered over.

Apart from them, for decades no one visited the Antarctic except a few intrepid scientists.

It was the world's last most romantic wilderness.

I planned to write a book about Antarctica. Beryl Bainbridge beat me to it. The moment her novel *The Birthday Boys*, about Scott's 1910 expedition, was announced, I knew two things – that my own book would never be written, and that something of the magic of the place I had held on to had died. Not Beryl's fault, of course.

But somehow it was still a secret, private, empty, desolate, fascinating, magical place, in my heart and mind. My rows of books grew.

Recently I was flicking through a magazine which had a 'Best Travel Destinations' supplement. I came upon Seabourn Cruises to the Antarctic. Then I had a call from friends saying they had just returned from an 'adventure holiday in Antarctica'.

The small secret flame went out at that moment, and today I packed up twenty-seven books about the white continent and took them to the charity shop.

————•○•————

JOHN KEATS WROTE in 'La Belle Dame Sans Merci' that 'The sedge has withered from the lake,/And no birds sing'.

No birds sing now. When they wind down and fall gradually silent, once all their nesting is done, the year starts to wither like the sedge and we are into the worst two months of the year, July and August. I know that for some these are for holidays and a general out-of-school feeling, but I have always disliked them. I hate everyone being on holiday, only at the end of email messages saying 'I am on annual leave'. The glory of not being bound by school terms and office hours is that one can take holidays whenever one fancies.

But it is the morning silence that is so depressing. Birds sing for a purpose. Once that has been fulfilled, I suppose they say stuff the rest of us, who fancy that they sing for our pleasure.

THOSE REQUESTS. They need to fill the pages of the weekend papers and colour magazines, so they send out questionnaires. Writers are asked questions on things like what book they wish they had written.

The answer could be anything one admires, and I always think it is preferable to choose a book one has not the faintest chance of having written, so magnificently beyond one's own capabilities is it, and that includes, of course, the works of Dickens, Thomas Hardy, P. G. Wodehouse, Virginia Woolf, Graham Greene ... But of all the novels I admire and whose author's talent I envy, the one I most often name is Ford Madox Ford's *The Good Soldier*. I have read it and re-read it and it is like a puzzle that looks so simple but is fiendish to unravel. How does he do the movement between the present and the immediate past and the distant past and the future, and back again, all smoothly, without a ruffle? How does he manage to deceive the reader by making the narrator apparently so truthful, only for us to realise he is the deceiver, and self-deceiver, of all fiction. It is so subtle and intricate and I long to work it all out.

There is plenty of commentary to read about *The Good Soldier* and no one has written it better than Julian Barnes, who understands this sort of thing from his close familiarity with and expertise on the French novel, but even he cannot really lay bare the workings, as one might the mechanism of a watch.

I tried to read more Ford. I have no interest left in the First World War, particularly in fiction about it, since having written *Strange Meeting* – what was an obsession is now quite dead. So I have not even tried *Parade's End*. It was adapted for television a few years ago, so, as always happens, the novels had a brief revival, but I wonder if it was a false dawn for F. M. Ford. Certainly, I have never known anyone who has read his trilogy, *The Fifth Queen*, about Katharine Howard.

In his lifetime he was famous for both founding and editing influential literary magazines, being an important figure on the contemporary book scene, and for his private life. Among other liaisons, he had an affair with Jean Rhys and was responsible for promoting her early work, before they fell out. None of these things, especially the latter, are of much interest now. Ford surely stands by *The Good Soldier*. It is a perfect example of a book which has achieved immortality for itself alone. If it contains elements of autobiography, these seem to be quite irrelevant today. Barnes says that 'He is not so much a writer's writer (which can suggest hermeticism) as a proper reader's writer. *The Good Soldier* needs The Good Reader.'

Now there is something I need to think about. What is a good reader? Attentive, obviously. I am not sure if it means one who reads slowly, because you can be so caught up in a book that you read on faster and faster, and not only because it's a thriller and you want to find out what happens. A good reader is definitely a thoughtful one – thinks about what has been read, goes over its meaning, anticipates. Is attentive, fully committed to and involved with the book. It is possible to be very detached from what one is reading, which may be appropriate occasionally but with fiction is surely not. A good reader pays attention to everything. The surface of the prose. The structure of the book. The tense. The point of view. Perhaps to those even before the characters. Then comes the setting. The story can often come last.

But is that just me?

The genius Nabokov has many enlightening things to say about it. Nabokov, the hero, who explained to me why, ultimately, Jane Austen is not as good as she is cracked up to be, and why, ultimately, Dickens is better (than Jane Austen, and than he is cracked up to be.) The book is *Lectures on Literature*, the chapter is 'Good Readers and Good Writers'. There are so many pertinent phrases and paragraphs, which go a long way towards clarifying one's thinking, so many ideas which, once read, seem obvious – but if that were the case, why have I not had them myself? Good reading is always re-reading, he says, partly because the first time one is anxious to find out what happens next – even in the most literary of novels. But also, the first time one is hard at work simply making the eyes move from left to right over unfamiliar prose: 'the very process of learning in terms of space and time what the book is about, this stands between us and artistic appreciation'.

He has a point, and the point makes me think, but it does not give me the lightning flash of illumination that this does, a page or two later: 'Literature was born, not the day when a boy came crying wolf, wolf out of the Neanderthal valley with a big gray wolf at his heels: literature was born on the day when a boy came crying wolf, wolf and there was no wolf behind him.'

I have continued to think about that ever since I first read it, ten or more years ago.

It is the same with Nabokov on Dickens's *Bleak House*, the best piece of criticism and explanation I have ever read on either author or novel. You will not encounter the same book you once knew if you re-read *Bleak House* after reading his elucidation.

Time to re-read Nabokov again. I have not got on with all of his fiction, but *Ada or Ardor* captured me when I was young, and *Pnin* in older age, and both left their marks in permanent ink. I mentioned a re-reading of the latter on Twitter. Sarah Churchwell tweeted back, 'I bloody love *Pnin*.'

I bloody do, too.

———•○•———

THESE ARE SAD, LIMP, GREY, mild days and the year has turned.

———•○•———

I DEBATE WITH MYSELF AGAIN. Is it better for someone not to read any books at all than to read only schlock/rubbish/badly written junk … whatever you like to call it? Is it better for young people to read nothing at all than read graphic novels – which are really only comics for an older age group? I argue to and fro, ping-pong, pong-ping.

Might the enjoyment of reading rubbish lead to an enjoyment of rather better books? It might. Or not.

Might graphic sci-fi lead to … or …

Does it matter? Is it better to be out in the fresh air or having a fun social life than mugging indoors reading low-grade porn or badly written uber-violent crime novels?

Probably. Yes.

Is reading a book a good, beneficial activity, per se?

Yes and yes.

But so many people simply cannot see the point.

AUGUST

APPLES AND PEARS AND PLUMS. 'What's for apple tonight?' Yes, it's a glut this summer. Once everyone is tired of picking and hauling them in, and eating yet more apple crumble, the rest fall and lie in the grass for the birds. Blackbirds love apples. A dozen will be gathered at once, pecking away.

It is hot.

———•◦•———

I READ AN ONLINE COMMENT about a book I have just finished. The author of the comment did not enjoy the novel. I did. But something about the book niggled and I could not work out what. The commentator said that in the end it 'didn't amount to anything'.

That switched on the light. That was what, ultimately, I had found unsatisfying about it and why I find a number of novels of its kind highly enjoyable, but in the end they do not 'amount to anything'.

The book in question was a Man Booker winner, Eleanor Catton's *The Luminaries*, set in the eighteenth century on the South Island of New Zealand. It is a long book and I devoured it. It is original, exciting, funny, mysterious ... a damn good story, with a whole array of wildly idiosyncratic characters. But although a terrific read, it did not touch the sides and has left little trace. It was a book I did not think about for a moment after I had finished it, but I suspect the author intended that I should. (That is not always the case. Not many detective novels or average thrillers leave a trace, and the authors would not expect them to.) The same is true of that one-time mega bestseller, Susanna Clarke's *Jonathan Strange & Mr Norrell*, which was televised very badly a couple of years back. Another book in which you immerse yourself and read breathlessly, but which again doesn't really amount to anything.

They have something in common, these books. Add to them *The Quincunx* by Charles Palliser. They are set in a fantasy period of history, or concern fantasy creatures, or a fantastic array of magic, or else they pick up on some things that actually happened, what was 'real', and play with them, moving them on world upon worlds away. They are bewitching and beguiling and fun, and there is nothing whatsoever wrong with that and I am not sneering. But they still do not really 'add up to anything'.

So what does? I recently re-read *The Sense of an Ending*, the Julian Barnes novel which won the 2011 Man Booker Prize, for which I was a judge. The Barnes was my choice. It was the almost-unanimous choice of the panel. It is a slim book – Barnes is not one to turn out 700 pages. But within its short space it contains truth, beauty, sadness, shrewdness, observation, intelligence, poignancy, self-pity, a man's coming to terms with his past ... everything one can think of about the human condition and more. And it amounts to a great deal. As do all of Barnes's novels. As do those of, shall we say, Kazuo Ishiguro and Zadie Smith and Anita Brookner and Penelope Fitzgerald – and several of them do not write at great length.

So now I have another criterion by which to assess fiction, after building up a collection of them over many years. Or perhaps they simply categorise it. Books which may be beautifully, brilliantly written and reveal a powerful, fantastic imagination at work, not to mention an author who knows how to transmute research into something else. But which, even so, do not ultimately add up to anything.

—•◦•—

THAT THINGS HAVE CHANGED in the writing/publishing/book world is a truism. Of course they have. Things should change, move forward, improve, progress, however we put it, in any area of life or business. Some of the changes are too obvious to note – the results of the new technology. Some have come about by osmosis. Some have happened as a knock-on effect of other changes.

But one thing has changed in the last, what, ten years. It has to do with the effect on a writer – and I am thinking primarily of novelists – of a sudden success at the very start of their careers. It is multi-factorial but recently, partly as the result of prizes and their hype, the book trade has been ravenously looking for new blood. New names. New writers. First-timers. This is why agents and publishers are all trawling graduate lists of the (many) schools of creative writing, why they are doing a sort of milk-round, in the way banks and major industries used to visit universities to woo their best graduates.

It works like this. A young CW graduate has written a novel which wins one of the university departmental prizes. An agent asks to see the novel, is impressed by ... something ... original-ity, fine writing, the wow factor – whatever. Agent takes on new author and soon hypes the novel among publishers, several of whom ask to see it and start bidding for it against one another. Because the rule always is that you may not want something until someone else indicates an interest in having it and then you want it *desperately*. The novel is bought for a decent – but not ridiculously large – sum and the publisher spreads the word about it excitedly. The novel is submitted for some of The Prizes, and gets on to one or two longlists. Then shortlists. And finally, perhaps, it wins something. Winning something changes everything – for a time. The author gets noticed, interviewed, attended to, the book is reviewed – whereas it might well not have been, had it failed to win something. People start tweeting about it. Booksellers recommend (aka 'hand-sell') it and soon it gets into the bestseller charts. Even though the entry may not actually represent massive sales, it is being in the charts that counts.

So far so great. And then our novelist is expected to write the follow-up. The second novel is always hard. Expectations for them have always run high. My second novel was a disaster and should never have seen the light of day, but the first had garnered a lot of publicity and general media attention, and I was very young.

The writer of a successful, heavily promoted prize-winning first novel now has the weight of everyone's expectations on their shoulders and these may prove fatal. Ideas do not come. Or bad ideas come. What would have been rejected by the writer, when working away in obscurity, as being not good enough, is now snatched at – there *must* be a second great idea, there has to be. Publisher, agent, booksellers, even readers ask all the time how it is getting on. In the past if it had not been getting on at all, perhaps even for three or five or seven years, nobody would have worried, the second book would have come when it was good and ready. But now? Now it has to come and soon. Already, this year's new young graduates and first-timers are biting at the heels of last year's, agents are back at the universities, the prize judges have been announced.

So, our author writes book two. It may be very good. It may be way better than book one. Or it may not. But if it does not get on to those longlists and shortlists, if it does not somehow become talked about again, if it does not garner a swathe of good reviews plus quotes from the Famous Established Novelists, if … then from the dizzy heights of those lists and the 60,000 sales, our novelist's second book may achieve sales of 2,000 if it's lucky. No one talks about it. The reading public has not rushed out to buy it. It sinks without trace. This is bad for the ego and the career of our first-timer, and is all too common. The agents and publishers and bookshops and reviewers and gossip columnists and readers have moved on to the Next Big Thing. There is only so much book-spending money each reader has – so they will buy the new novel by X, a long- established favourite, or by the latest prize winner, and … and that's it. Poor old first-timer. Shattered dreams, a stalled career, instead of having one that builds slowly – and no one takes their calls.

Meanwhile, the long-established Good Novelist, who has won the prizes and the plaudits in the past, has just published their twenty-fourth novel. And it is fine. It is respectable – no, it is better than that, but the problem is that it sells roughly the same number of copies as the last one and the one before that. It doesn't break new ground, does not surprise, does not challenge. And the author is sixty-plus. And … 'Well, I'm sorry, but your sales have been slipping, and of course the new young booksellers haven't heard of you and may even think you're already dead and … and everyone is talking about this new young writer who has just come out of a creative writing course and anyway, the manuscript you have sent me is a bit too much like the last – and the one before that and the one before …'

What is the answer? There isn't one, except that our older writer needs to pull her socks up, do something different, startle them, change pace, change genres, surprise, delight … or give up. Go quietly on her own terms, not on those of the others.

The over-hyped young novelist with such a massive success the first time and near-oblivion the second? They have to get on quietly with a really good book, discarding any ideas which are not starred first-class, forgetting everyone and everything except the writing. They have to write without expectations but with ambition, they have to write in obscurity, understanding that unless they come up with the goods, and better than the goods, again, they will be nowhere. If they are the real thing, then sooner or later they will indeed come up to expectation. They will be building the foundations of a solid career.

If I am asked for advice I always say, 'Don't give up the day job', no matter what it is, because however well your first book did, however large a sum of money you may have made, one swallow does not make a summer or one successful book a long and lucrative career.

———●○●———

Outside the moon is up – the harvest moon over harvest fields. It casts a sheen upon the empty stubbles, the bare rounding slopes, so altered from the close-crowded landscape of standing corn. It has glimmering secrets among the trees, and pierces itself into every entanglement of foliage, and lays faint shadows across the paths. Each finds a ghost of himself beside him on the ground. An elusive radiance haunts the country; the distances have a sense of shining mist. The men move homeward from the field; the last load creaking up the hill behind them, the hoofs of the horses thudding, their breath sounding short. Peace comes, a vision in the fairy armour of moonlight, the peace of 'man goeth forth unto his work until the evening' …

I WISH I HAD WRITTEN THAT. It is from *Corduroy*, the first book of a trilogy about Suffolk country life before the last war by Adrian Bell. He was another who used to write a column for the *EDP*, a farmer, an observer, a lover of nature and deeply, intimately knowledgeable about his county and its rural ways of life. They have almost all gone now, but in my lifetime, I was staying in Wiltshire during harvest and we all loaded the bales on to the binder and cold drinks were brought round. Twenty years later, living in an Oxfordshire village, I stood at our gate to watch the tractors as they came groaning up the lane, pulling their load of hay in the moonlight. Those are still to be seen today. The tractors come laden past this gate. Once, when this was a farm, they would have turned in to where I am standing. Yet in some ways, nothing changes. There are no working horses, of course, but tractors round here are not all vast and shiny and as expensive as a house, some are good old sturdy workhorses, decades old. Farmers cannot afford to replace them as we replace our cars and they are all expert motor engineers, keeping the machinery moving, even if it means an emergency running repair with bailer twine.

Adrian Bell's *Corduroy*, together with its successors, *Silver Ley* and *The Cherry Tree*, is a record of farming life written by an outdoors person who had a poet's eye and pen. As a young man in London, indeed, Bell had begun writing successful poetry, but his father sent him, as a wet-behind-the-ears townie, to Mr Colville in Suffolk to see if he had the makings of a farmer. He did and was good at it. He enjoyed it, but he was still – perhaps first of all – a writer.

Bell's books go in and out of print, but there are often second-hand copies available inexpensively. Mine sit on the kitchen shelf where local history and topography and suchlike go, next to Lilias Rider Haggard and another, rather more recent East Anglian writer, Ronald Blythe, author of *Akenfield*. Blythe has the gift of turning a phrase so crisply, with such an individual tone, that one re-reads a sentence or two over and over again, for the sheer pleasure of rolling the words in the mouth. Inevitably, one then remembers it. Here he is writing about a visiting choir, come from a nearby town for a local choral festival: 'They are princely in scarlet, and can sing. It is a known fact. They loll against our tombstones.' It is the words 'princely' and 'loll' which do it – somehow this short sentence conveys the lofty air of the visitors, and the innate sense of superiority of the hosts – they are, after all, 'our' tombstones.

———•○•———

TOO HOT FOR ME. The dog and cat seek the shade and only the blasted pigeons make a sound.

———•○•———

A FRIEND SAYS she is lost without her book group, which does not meet in August. Not against book groups – how could any writer be, though I could never belong to one. But they make people read books when they might not, and read better ones than they might otherwise. It depends on the group, of course. I went to speak to one in Oxfordshire whose next choice was *The Odyssey* and after that A *Pilgrim's Progress*, before they returned to contemporary fiction and *Midnight's Children*.

Another friend writes that she has given up on fiction because she finds new novels either pretentious and sub-James Joycean, or junk. She reads non-fiction instead, mainly about wild life and country life and the history of the landscape. I alternate but I never give up on fiction for long, even if it is the classics only for a few months. It's just the way the wind blows me. I wish I could read fat historical biographies and books about battles, though I am not sure why. The only history that really absorbs me is of the twelfth century and, lately, about Society and aristocratic women in the twentieth. One leads to another. The medieval monks write on parchment, shear their sheep, construct an elaborate drainage system, pray and fast. The satin-clad, Marcel-waved, cigarette-holder gels turn into ambulance drivers and secret agents in wartime.

The Raj is of never-ending fascination, too, but that can equally well be fiction. Paul Scott's *Raj Quartet* never fails and it has the ring of truth. Ootacamund must be full of ghosts. The hills – a paradise for birds. And scorpions. Scorpions. Suddenly I fly from the Raj to Corfu and the story of how Gerry Durrell kept his scorpions in a matchbox and how his brother Larry opened it inadvertently … 'It's that bloody boy again!' That sends me running to the shelf where my battered copy of *My Family and*

Other Animals lives. Some books here should really be replaced with new, but the battered old ones read best, I find.

———•◦•———

THE SWIFTS HAVE GONE. The saddest moment has been and gone, the one when you realise the skies are empty overhead and know there is such a wait until they arrive again next May, and then only for such a brief stay – though not quite as brief as that of the cuckoo. Swifts belong to one of the most ancient of bird groups, the Apodidae, and they are long-lived, as small birds go. They are monogamous and the same pair will breed together in successive years. They may spend two or three years on the wing before breeding and making a nest, they sleep on the wing and are the only birds known to mate on it, too.

But they do not bear the best Latin name for a bird. That is surely the one for the wren. *Troglodytes troglodytes*.

———•◦•———

I HAVE NEVER READ ANYTHING by Ursula Le Guin because she writes fantasy and science fiction and I do not enjoy reading either, though as a child I certainly loved fantasy. Most children do. Perhaps a lot of us just grow out of it, although I know that many do not. Sci fi is somewhat, though not totally, different. Some people only ever read science fiction. They are obsessive. They may go to congresses and conferences and fan gatherings. A lot of them are men. It is a strange and entirely harmless world and it gives much harmless pleasure but I just cannot suspend my disbelief enough to want to join them. I have tried, Heaven knows, but never got beyond one third of a book.

I enjoy discovering what other writers think, though, about writing, literature, the world, politics and even *Troglodytes troglodytes*. I search out collections of essays in which I may find all these things and more. Ursula Le Guin's fiction may not be to my taste but when I came upon her *Words are My Matter* I bought it. She talks a lot of sense, though she is annoying when she bangs one drum over and over – in complaints against commercial publishers, present-day publishing, and the general decline of both. She also hates chain booksellers and regards them as mere pushers of product, without interest or knowledge of literature or love of books. She is wrong about that, at least in this country (Le Guin is American). Most of the staff I have encountered in various branches of the largest chain bookseller in the UK have been passionate and informed readers, anxious to lead their customers to something new and delightful. Quite a few of them have become published writers themselves. (The only chain of shops whose staff are entirely ignorant of and uninterested in the books they stock mainly sells stationery, confectionary, newspapers and magazines.)

But Le Guin has some pertinent and intelligent things to say about her own chosen genre of fiction, and about genre fiction in general. Every writer and reader (and bookseller) should be required to read her chapter on this subject.

The trouble with opposing Litfic to Genrefic is that what looks like a reasonable distinction of varieties of fiction hides an unreasoned value judgment – Lit superior, Genre inferior. This is mere prejudice. We must have a more intelligent discussion of what literature is …

To get out of this boring bind, I propose an hypothesis:

Literature is the extant body of written work.
All novels belong to it.

Her next point flows from this simple but all-encompassing distinction. There is, she says, a real mystery which we can work at to try and solve, every time we read a book.

Why is one book entertaining, another disappointing, another a rev-
elation and a lasting joy? What is quality? What makes a good book
good and a bad book bad?
    Not its subject. Not its genre. What, then? That's what good
book criticism, good book talk, has always been about.

I wonder, though, how much of this is subjective, even if we get past the 'I liked the hero' and 'I don't like novels written in the present tense'. Of course, academic literary criticism is not subjective – or it would like us to think that it is not.

------•◦•------

GLORIOUS TWELFTH?

Rough shooting is one thing, part of the farming way of life, which is as much about conservation as anything – and of course was always a way of hunter man feeding himself and his family. But driven pheasant shooting – killing thousands of birds which have been reared only for the shoot, and which are later two a penny at the butchers, so that a large percentage of those shot are just buried in a pit – that is another matter. Grouse shooting is a little better, but not much. I enjoy roast pheasant but could never stomach grouse again after I learned how many red worms its body contains. But those who would ban country sports do not understand that simply to leave everything untouched, unculled and allowed to breed unchecked, would be a far worse cruelty, would cause the destruction by neglect of much of the country and shrink the rural economy rapidly. And a good shot ensures that a bird dies a very quick death.

———•○•———

THIS IS THE TIME OF YEAR when the book trade starts to gear up for the autumn rush. There are more new titles published in September and October than in any other months, most of them aimed at Christmas buyers. The Man Booker Prize longlist appears at the end of July, then the shortlist in September, with the winner announced in October, to send everyone into a frenzy. The Costa Book Awards and several lesser ones come at the end of this year or the beginning of next. All of them hike sales of new books, which, whatever else one may think of prizes, can't be a bad thing.

I always wait until at least a year after any of the prizes before reading those on the lists which appeal. It is amazing how everything settles down and finds its natural level. Hype never did any reader much good.

———•○•———

SHIRLEY HAZZARD AGAIN. I could start a Hazzard quote-a-day:

The attempt to touch truth through a work of imagination requires an inner center of privacy and solitude. We all need silence – both external and interior – in order to find out what we truly think.

Just finished the Ursula Le Guin essays, too. Here is a very handy quote for other writers:

But please don't ask me where I get my ideas from. I have managed to keep the address of the company where I buy my ideas a secret all these years, and I'm not about to let people in on it now.

Of all the opening lines I envy and remember with glee every so often, perhaps this is the one that makes me smile: 'One day in my young youth at high summer, lolling with my lovely companions upon a haystack, I found a needle' – Muriel Spark, 'The Portobello Road'.

————•○•————

I SUPPOSE WE WILL NEVER, until the end of time, stop the knee-jerk comments about the 2011 Man Booker Prize, for which I was a judge, together with Dame Stella Rimington, Gaby Wood, Chris Mullin and Matthew d'Ancona. It has gone into folklore as the year the judges were of inferior and 'populist' quality, who had not a clue about literature. I read that I was 'supremely unqualified' for the task. I do wonder how else I might have improved my chances of being qualified. I have a first class honours degree in English from King's College, London; I have published over fifty books, including several prize-winning novels; I have been a regular reviewer of fiction in a wide variety of newspapers and journals since 1963; I introduced a TV book programme, presented BBC Radio 4's *Bookshelf* and *A Good Read*; and I have been not only a previous Booker Prize judge but a judge for every other major fiction prize. In what way was I 'unqualified'?

The rest were a mixture: a leading journalist and former editor of the *Spectator*; the then literary editor of the *Daily Telegraph*; a politician and former MP who had written some very well received memoirs; and the former head of MI5, who is one of the best-read women I have ever met. The literary director of the Booker Foundation, Ion Trewin, who knew more about the book scene and literary prizes than anyone living, selected us.

We worked very hard, we read over 120 novels. But, because these things are always chance, it was not a vintage year for literary fiction. We had an awful lot of poor stuff to wade through, but wade we did, and our discussions – aka arguments – were long, fierce and passionate. It was not easy to compile a longlist of novels we all felt were worthy, and if the criterion was, as it must be, that every book included was a potential winner of the prize, then we failed because, hands on hearts, we did not feel that one or two of our longlist choices were worthy of winning. That was, again, because of the low-ish standard of that particular year's entries.

But when it came to the shortlist, we had no doubts. Our arguments were just as passionate, but really the shortlisted novels chose themselves. So far so good. But then we came to the announcement of the shortlist, which is always at a press conference. No problem there. We had no agenda and, of course, the winner is only chosen on the day of the prize dinner. But some members of the assembled press corps clearly did have an agenda, and one of the first questions was, Had we failed to put on our shortlist the novel by Alan Hollinghurst because he was a homosexual? Stella Rimington would have refused to answer such a question on principle, and Chris Mullin confessed that he had not even known that Hollinghurst was a gay man. Matthew, Gaby and

I did know but felt that it was totally irrelevant. We were choosing a book, a novel, not an author for his or her sexuality. It was a shocking accusation.

Still, we might have got through unscathed, had one member of the press pack not asked the perfectly legitimate question about what had been our criteria for selecting the shortlist. Chris Mullin answered first, for no special reason, but what he said was our downfall and will haunt us all for the rest of our days. He said that what he had been looking for was that they had to 'zip along'. Which of course was translated as 'an easy read', which became 'something popular', and so on, and so on.

I do not know why Chris used that phrase. I know what he was trying to say, but for it to 'zip along' is not one of my litmus tests for a great novel. But there it was. It stuck. It scuppered our chances of being taken seriously. It scuppered everything. We have gone down in book history as a bunch of lightweights who had no business being asked to judge a prize for literary fiction. Judging by some of the comments you would think we were all barely literate.

Our winner, which was a not-quite but nearly unanimous choice, was Julian Barnes's fine novel *The Sense of an Ending*, which improves with each re-reading, as Barnes always tends to do. Nobody complained. Everyone in the room at the dinner was happy. The book sold in huge quantities. But we will still never live our reputation as the 'zip along' judges down. Ironically, the last time I saw Chris Mullin was at the memorial service for Ion Trewin. He was a bit rueful.

SEPTEMBER

THIS GARDEN IS IN SOUTH-WEST FRANCE. The house is small and the garden is large, with old, shady trees and places where comfortable chairs and small tables have been set out of the sun. They are for snoozing, for sitting out over a glass of wine. For reading. There is a deep covered terrace, too, with sofas and chairs. Another reading spot.

I am not a sun-worshipper and it has been very hot, so I have followed the shade with my book, under the trees, which have not yet begun to turn. It is very still. There has not been the faintest breeze, for days. The three cats belonging to the main house stay inside, or in dark places beneath shrubs, until evening. The three red hens do the same.

I have brought a heavy book bag, as usual, but, also as usual, in the rented cottage there is a small bookcase packed with other people's left-behinds.

They fascinate me, those holiday reads, and I have studied a good many in my time. Indeed, I have compiled a list of the authors whose books – always in paperback – are most often found in rented properties, both at home and here in France. I start going through them as soon as I have unpacked and I rarely score fewer than five.

The list does change every few years.

This year the bookcases have contained, in no particular order:

Joanna Trollope *

Dan Brown

Jenny Colgan

Stephen King *

Daphne du Maurier

Victoria Hislop *

Ian McEwan *

Val McDermid *

P. D. James *

Ruth Rendell *

Jojo Moyes *

And *Gone Girl* and *The Girl on the Train*. *Captain Corelli's Mandolin* has not been found for a while.

The asterisk means that those authors are in this year's house.

Several authors dropped off the bottom a couple of years ago – Catherine Cookson, Dean Koontz, Gerald Durrell, Peter Mayle. John le Carré comes and goes.

This year there are a few surprises. Olivia Manning's *Balkan Trilogy* is here. So are books by Julian Barnes, Martin Amis, Elizabeth Bowen, Patricia Highsmith, Jeanette Winterson – and Jane Austen, Dickens, Charlotte Brontë, Hemingway and Raymond Carver. An upmarket bookcase, then.

Serendipitously, I have brought both Olivia Manning trilogies, and it is those I have started reading – or rather, re-reading – with a break in the middle for two novels by Edith Wharton.

In between *those*, because this is how I always read, I am catching up, decades late, on Jay McInerney and *Brightness Falls*, one of the American 'Brat Pack' novels, about the young turks of New

York finance and publishing, who rose to dizzy heights before coming a cropper a few years ago. It is very sharp, very witty and it includes a comment about holiday reading, when the Bright Young Couple go to a paradise island.

> *'This is vacation,' she said. 'You should read something really trashy.' They combed through the musty-smelling swollen paperbacks and Reader's Digest condensed novels on the living-room shelves.*

In other words, beach reads. I was slightly mortified when a friend on holiday in Turkey reported seeing three people reading one of my crime novels on a beach – I have never taken them too seriously, but for a split second I thought, 'I didn't realise they were as bad as that.'

The Olivia Manning trilogies have grown in stature since they were first published – as some books do. They have already stood the test of time and I am sure they will go on doing so, while novels by many of her female contemporaries have all sunk without trace. Ivy Compton-Burnett anyone? Kay Dick?

There are plenty of Second World War novels, and more pour off the presses with every year that takes us away from 1939, but Manning does not touch the Battle of Britain or the Blitz. In fact, she barely mentions England at all. The six novels are set in Romania – *The Balkan Trilogy* – and Egypt –*The Levant Trilogy*, because this is where Olivia Manning and her husband Reggie Smith spent their own war. They are the models for Guy and Harriet Pringle, who, like them, met and married in haste at the beginning of the war and spent much of it in the Balkans and the Levant. Reggie Smith, like Guy Pringle in the novels, works for the British Council and his wife, although getting occasional jobs in foreign legations, spends much of her time exploring the cities in which she finds herself, and travelling occasionally out of them, to villages, seaside resorts and the pyramids, and socialising, perforce, in cafés and bars while waiting for her husband to come home to the various rented flats and rooms, which are variously uncomfortable and sometimes squalid. Harriet never complains about the war or the conditions in which she finds herself, but she half-complains about the way her husband has time and attention for anyone and everyone before he can spare any for her.

This summer's re-reading must be my fourth, and each time the books yield something new, perhaps because as I grow older I understand more. They give the sense of countries and cities at war more vividly than any other English literature I know – the smells, the noises, the deprivations, the sudden panics, the ominous lulls, the atmospheres of cafés and hotels, the temporary nature of every relationship – which makes them all the more vivid and fervid – all of these things fill the novels with detail. I have never visited Romania or Egypt, and have certainly never been near a desert, yet I feel, via Manning's books, that I know them and in a strange way have always known them. Manning said often that she could not invent anything, that her novels were descriptions of her own experience, but that cannot be altogether true.

In *The Levant Trilogy* two brothers in their early twenties are serving with the British army in the desert. One is killed. The other serves and fights on, is later wounded and hospitalised, apparently paraplegic. Their relationship is briefly described, and we never encounter them together, yet we understand the depth of their brotherly feeling and the agony of the one left behind. We are there, we know intimately what this sort of war was like in physical detail. We feel the extreme heat, the sandstorms blowing up in front of us, so that we taste the stuff, it gets into our eyes and lungs, we smell death and blood, we see the enemy ahead – or is that the enemy, through the heat shimmer, and not another brigade of our own force? How can we tell? The chaos and muddle of this war, the commands and counter-commands, the guess-work, the attempts to find out what the hell is going on a mile ahead, let alone in the rest of the battlefield, or the entire theatre of war – these are wonderfully conveyed. Manning was a more imaginative and creative a novelist than she knew, for all that so much of her own experience and so many of the people taken from life are part of the weft and warp of the books.

I sat for a long time at the end of the day's reading, as the sun set and the air cooled and the night scents and smells rose from the garden, thinking and thinking about these novels. I had probably done this thinking, or a version of it, several times before but the books had given me more to brood about. It is seventy plus years since those days through which we live in the two war trilogies. Olivia Manning died in 1980. I wonder if it matters how much she wrote out of her own direct experience and how much she created from her imagination – 'made up'.

Does it *ever* matter? Only at the time, perhaps. A decade, or half a century later, it is all one. The books stand or fall by them-selves. That is what time does to literature. And these novels stand. They come up fresh at every re-reading. I laid down the last as I finished it and sat in the soft dusk, with moths batting against the lamp and owls hooting somewhere deep in the French woods, and felt moved all over again, and made to think what it had been like for my parents' generation, and the one before, and for those so-young soldiers in the desert – the Boulderstone brothers are twenty and twenty-two, the age at which young men now are still boys to us. In the war they had to grow up fast. You were an officer, men called you 'Sir' and looked to you for orders and leadership and you were still celebrating your twenty-first birthday.

Olivia Manning was an unusual-looking young woman, with a pointed face and a large nose, but as she grew older her face became softer and less strange. She was a difficult person, hard-working, knowing her own worth as a writer but always feeling that she did not get her just deserts, in the form of praise and prizes, but was constantly overlooked in favour either of the new posse of 'Angry Young Men' or of the other women novelists she saw as rivals. She was dismissive about most of them, not because she really believed their books were poor so much as because she was jealous of them. She need not have been.

A chip on the shoulder is always unattractive and, in her day, I sometimes heard Olivia being mocked by her contemporaries. My friend Pamela Hansford Johnson admired her work and spoke up for it, and the admiration was mutual. Mention Iris Murdoch or Muriel Spark, though, and Olivia became enraged that they both received such adulatory attention from the literary editors – who were in those days always men. (Come to think of it, most of them still are.) She was furious that every time one of Murdoch's long novels appeared it was what she called 'Iris Benefit Week', and she loathed Spark as being too smart, too fashionable, too laden with jewellery. Too rich. She was wrong about her fiction, though. Novels like *The Prime of Miss Jean Brodie, The Comforters, The Girls of Slender Means* are very different from anything Olivia wrote, but they still yield a great deal today. Her style is very – well, stylish. Perhaps an acquired taste. Her wit is straight-faced and very Morningside. Her characters are almost but not quite carica-tures. She was not trying, as Olivia was, to write realistic novels, she was doing something quite different. And doing it brilliantly. And her short stories are impeccable – perfect examples of what the short story does and the novel does not.

Iris Murdoch is another matter. I have tried to re-read her books but only one, to my mind, has lasted – *The Bell*, a master-piece of irony and extremely funny. I have re-read it often and recommended it, successfully, to people who say they cannot take Murdoch. Otherwise, her odd fantasy-cum-philosophical castles-in-the-air are hard to take now. They have dated, though they are set in some out-of-time period which is supposedly England after the war but never seems to be quite anytime or anywhere. I doubt if she will ever have her day again. She was too donnish, too clever, took herself too seriously as a writer. But I knew and liked her. And something else about Iris has just struck me. Perhaps it was just chance, but I never ever heard her speak a bad word about any of her contemporaries. Maybe she just hadn't read their novels, but that doesn't stop some people.

Olivia Manning's books stand tall alongside any one by those who, like her, were writing in the second half of the twentieth century, and above quite a few. She was a great writer. Her books were given a shot in the arm when *The Balkan Trilogy* was tele-vised as *The Fortunes of War*, starring Kenneth Branagh and Emma Thompson, at the end of the 1980s. But the boost of a TV adaptation to book sales is short-lived and a new appreciation of Olivia Manning's work is long overdue. Her other novels deserve attention but the war trilogies are the very best of her, and just as it does not matter that they were in part autobiographical, so her own prickly persona is of no interest to the newcomer to her work in the twenty-first century.

I cannot think that even now I have now done with the *Balkan* and *Levant* trilogies. In ten years' time, I am sure I will pick them up again and find more meaning in them. Most great books yield their full meaning slowly

It is getting late. The moths are pattering against the lamps. This French garden smells of night and autumn. I blow out the citronella candle, and go indoors.

AT THE FAR END OF THE GARDEN is an old stone animal shelter, and behind it has been put a wicker chair which is probably almost as old. It has deep cushions that have been well bedded-in and after about three o'clock the shade slips over and covers it and I sit reading there. When I look up, there is a sloping meadow where the stubble is waiting to be ploughed, next to a field full of sun-flowers – an important crop down here. They stay, heads hung, until they dry out and blacken, before being harvested. On the skyline, a row of oak trees. This area is rich in trees, and dense woods where wild boar hang out, and from which I can hear the sounds of hounds baying and yelping and guns during afternoons of *la chasse*. The French are great hunters, but not, like us, on horseback. I am not unhappy about the hunting of wild boar. Their numbers have to be kept down, they are predators, and they are dangerous. There are no boar in this garden, I hope. They will be hiding in the dark and cool of the woods.

My book bag contains a strange selection of books I have been waiting to read or re-read or am halfway through, but the heat has increased, it is humid and sultry – and that makes me irritable. No book will quite do. I wander into the house to go through the shelves there again. When I am in France I try to keep up my grasp of the language – such as it is – by reading *Le Figaro* and the local newspaper of the Lot every day, and sometimes a book in French. I bought a Simenon in the local *librairie*. But in this oppressive weather the words will not filter through into my brain.

I have brought all three of Edith Wharton's wonderful Old New York novels, which I turn to every five years or so. But until the inevitable thunderstorm breaks the weather, I will resort to what is called 'light reading'. That novel by Jay McInerney is on the table beside me. I had never previously read anything by him but my elder daughter raves and I love novels about New York, set at any time. I don't suppose the author would be pleased to have his book called 'light', but I can't quite think of another term – it is certainly not 'heavy'.

It is also the sort of novel one plunges into, as into the deep end of the pool, and swims off straight away. The prose is cool and observant, in that crisp American way, and I know what is going to happen, so there is the delightful build-up to the crisis. These young people, married, wife in finance, the husband in publishing, are going to experience life in New York as it crashes and burns. They are going to lose their jobs, fail to hang on to their apartment, suffer with their friends in the same worlds, the same boat … I love books where pride cometh before a fall. Schadenfreude rules. Is that bad? Yes, but not as bad as gleefully wishing the crash and decline on real people.

Nothing happens fast in this novel. I read fifty pages, before the sun moves round, and I am not much further forward, but McInerney's depiction of a self-regarding novelist who has been writing his 'great novel' for twenty years and endlessly getting his publisher to take him out to lunch in expensive and fashionable restaurants, to talk about the publicity for his non-novel, is spot on. I have met plenty of what Franz Kafka called non-writing writers. Have you ever heard of a non-painting painter or a non-composing composer? But those writers who never quite get on with their book are around – using 'block', the 'pram in the hall', the day job, anything – as a reason for never producing. Meanwhile, if they have done their self-publicity well, they are always referred to as 'X, the novelist' (note, 'the' not 'a') in interviews. '… as someone once said of E. M. Forster, his reputation grew with each book he failed to publish'. I have seen that happen, and not in New York.

McInerney knows them all. He also knows that a publishing house is only as good as its last bestseller, and how two or three books which do less than brilliantly can make all the difference between success and going under. The head of the firm for which our hero works has a habit of sending back curt notes about the manuscripts sent along by his editors. 'I can see these poems probably ought to be published, but why by us?'

This is the perfect holiday book, but it does not slip down like a bland drink. It is not a time-waster. It is not the kind of book you can't put down. I put it down quite often, in order to think about what I have just read. It is meaty and it creates a whole, real but fictional world. It has sharp observations, rapier-sharp dialogue. It is emphatically not a beach read, but reading it does not make my brain melt in the ambient temperature of 34 degrees.

———•O•———

THE WEATHER BREAKS. It has been unbearably humid as well as hot, and I am no good with it. Though it has been fine to sit in the shade, or outside on the terrace in the evenings, behind a wall of anti-mosquito coils and with pyrethrum-scented flesh, reading by a pleasantly wavering light. But there is still no breeze. Even the very tops of the elms do not stir.

Thunder is near. Sheet lightning flares. Something out there makes a strange cry.

When the storm comes, it is short and very sharp, but the rain will please the farmers, who have had none since late June. It rains all night, steadily, soothingly, and much of the next day, and the following night. Everything suddenly smells wonderful.

When it stops, the yellow-brown grass is greening already, and the heaviness has dissolved away, yielding to miraculously cool air – so cool it has dropped from 34 to 18 degrees in twenty-four hours. We look out jumpers and I read inside, sprawled on the comfortable sofa indoors until it warms gradually again, reaching the mid-20s but no longer oppressive.

Autumn is hovering close by. The trees are beginning to turn. The nights draw in. But still, I can be outside on this or that garden chair or wicker chaise longue, reading.

———•O•———

A CLATTERING LATE LAST NIGHT just outside the back door. We used to get badgers in the Cotswolds and Jeanette Winterson, who lived not far away, always swore they ate her crockery. But there are relatively few in Norfolk, so it wasn't that. The clattering continued. I went outside and found a hedgehog knocking the tin dog-food dish about. They are so rare now, though if ever a garden, and its environs, were attractive to them, this is it. We have wild areas and long grass and weedy areas, and heaps which were meant to be compost but never quite made it. All of these are supposedly attractive to hedgehogs. Once, coming back late, I had to slam on the brakes to spare a family of them marching down the lane ahead of me. So they are about.

I put out some meaty chunks from the cat food, refilled the water bowl and left it to itself. Everything went very quiet but the meat had gone in the morning. It might not, of course, have been taken by the hedgehog.

Children's books sometimes feature hedgehogs, though I daresay they are as weird and wonderful as dinosaurs to young readers. Mrs Tiggywinkle is the archetype. There is no hedgehog in *The Wind in the Willows*, though there ought to be. Fuzzypeg the Hedgehog is a friend of Little Grey Rabbit in the stories by Alison Uttley. And of course there is Sonic the Hedgehog, though he inhabits a game world not a book one.

OCTOBER

THE NEW ACADEMIC YEAR. When we lived in Oxford, schools had been back three weeks or so before the university term began and the city filled up with bicycles. It made a difference, mainly in the square mile where the principal colleges are. It used to make an even greater one when undergraduates wore gowns in town. It is a pity they wear them no longer, but Oxbridge got rid of them decades ago. When I was in London, at King's, only theologians and lawyers wore gowns. I longed for one but I have never worn an academic gown and, as I refuse all offers of honorary degrees, I am sure I never will.

———•◦•———

IN SUMMER THE VILLAGE smells of barbecues. Now it smells of bonfires and the first wood smoke curls up, drifting into my nostrils from a dozen chimneys. The wood man has been round several times, tipping trailer-loads of logs. Now, of course, we are told we should not be burning them. We gave up coal years ago. Oil became a dirty word. Environmentally friendly folk converted to biomass, at great expense, but apparently research has shown that this is just as bad as everything else. We are meant to put on more jumpers, I expect. Wrens just dive deep into thick bushes and cling together for warmth. There were at least three nests of them on the south side of the house this year and yesterday I saw one dive into the hawthorn, which is well sheltered by two old walls adjacent to it. And so, barring a bitter winter and many nights of sub-zero temperatures, *Troglodytes troglodytes* should be fine. I hope so. Such tiny, vulnerable birds. I picked up a dead one and there was nothing in my hand at all. Weightless as air.

———•O•———

SOME NOVELISTS SEEM to be ashamed of stories. Of telling stories. Of novels containing stories. Stories are the least of it, they seem to say, and if I have to have a story as a sort of coathanger on which to hang my coat of many coloured words, it will have to be thin and spare, plain and dull, a story no one will actually want to read, but they must bear with me because I am told that my novel must contain a story of some sort. Stories are what people like. Stories sell books.

The great novelists knew better. Imagine Dickens without any stories. What are Chaucer's *Canterbury Tales* but a series of linked stories? Where would Shakespeare be without the stories, even if Shaw did say that Shakespeare had the 'gift of telling a story (provided someone told it to him first)'.

Italo Calvino was a story genius. So was Nabokov. And they both believed in stories as others believe in God. They played with stories. Calvino's *If on a Winter's Night a Traveller*, one of the most playful, delightful and brilliant modern novels written, is all about stories. Only about stories: 'I'm producing too many stories, because what I want for you is to feel around the story, a saturation of other stories I could tell and maybe will tell or who knows may already have told on some other occasion ...' David Mitchell, in

Cloud Atlas, produced a novel in the Calvino mode, which is not to say that he plagiarised or copied the idea. A series of separate stories told and interwoven until they become one big story – that is really a literary form as old as literature itself.

'I can't be doing with that,' a friend said – a friend who reads a lot. 'I like to know where I am and who I am with, in a book. I don't like all this stopping and starting and changing about once I have settled into it.'

I know what she means. I like to know where I am in a novel, too. Sometimes. But just as a long straight road has its pleasures and its purposes, so does a series of winding, unexpected lanes which eventually converge, but which give you a lot of surprises on the way, even when they appear to come to dead ends.

————•○•————

WHEN I FIRST WENT TO LIVE IN LONDON, in 1960, and indeed for the next decade or more, there were no bookshop chains, other than WHSmith, which was not even then primarily a bookseller. There were no Waterstones, Daunts … But London had plenty of famous independent book shops with style and character: Bumpus, Truslove & Hanson, Foyles, with its almost impenetrable system of purchasing books by way of several chits and queues. The anarchic Better Books. The insanely anarchic Parton Bookshop, belonging to a man called David Archer, who seemed not to want to sell anything, and where writers drank coffee and talked and smoked and read books and nicked them.

Of course they are all gone, other than Foyles, whose present-day premises are like an ocean liner and whose system for purchasing has become normal. But there are plenty of bookshops with character, where you are likely to find both the obvious and the unexpected and where the stock is not arranged in uniform ranks, edge to edge, but presents something of a challenge to the browser. So long as the staff know where to put a hand on what you have come in for, a bit of disarrangement and disorganisation lends charm. There are no probably none left with histories and personalities, like 88 Charing Cross Road or Shakespeare & Co. in Paris, the stuff of legend, bookshops about which people wrote books. People still do travel great distances to particular bookshops, though. A friend journeyed from Devon specifically to check out Topping & Co. of Ely. She may still be in there.

The internet did not kill off bookshops, any more than the e-reader killed the physical book, though online antiquarian bookselling has dealt a mortal blow to many small second-hand shops. But poke around country towns and you can still find them, eccentric, idiosyncratic and only seeming, in the dusty chaos, to contain tremendous rare bargains for pence. The proprietors who lurk in their dim depths know their stock and its worth down to the last 1940s *Film Fun* annual.

———•○•———

'IT DRIVES ME MAD when David isn't reading,' the friend said. I wasn't sure what she meant, but apparently her husband has a binge on reading every evening, every night, on the commuter train, and for a couple of hours in bed on Sunday mornings. This lasts for several weeks, or even months, during which time he gets through dozens of books, mainly but not all non-fiction. And then he stops. He reads no book at all for weeks. Months. Once, for a whole year and a half.

How is this possible? How can one be an intermittent reader?

———— •○• ————

'THIRTY DAYS HATH SEPTEMBER ...'

Home again, and the trees are still green. It is mild, but an English dampness is in the air, the nights are chill, and every dawn and dusk fine veils of pale spooky mist weave over the surface of the river and the pond, a few feet above the ground. The apples are thumping down. Maybe it is time to re-read Laurie Lee and *Cider with Rosie*, but I can't find it, and there are plenty of the new autumn titles to look at and maybe even to read. Publishers are kind enough to send me all manner of books for nothing and I browse in our local bookshop and online to see what is predicted to be this year's Christmas bestseller. But the best-laid plans of publishers 'aft gang aglay' because those always come from left field, leaving printers burning the midnight oil to meet sudden massive demand. Last year, I remember, it was a book about how to chop and store logs.

———— •○• ————

A DECADE AGO I did what I had longed to do since 1963, when I received my first degree, and started to read for another, an MA this time, in theology. Having been brought up in a Catholic convent, and spent many years as an adult Anglican, particularly as a member of the Coventry Cathedral community, I felt – and indeed, still feel – that I knew too little about the basis of and background to it all and about various aspects of Christian history. But I wasn't about to return as a full-time student to what is now called the campus, I studied by distance learning. If you have already taken a first degree, and especially if you are older and doing this voluntarily, and so anxious to learn and put the hours in, this is an ideal way. The internet has made it all possible. My essays were e-mailed in and marked and returned by the same route, but nice, fat, printed books of the modules came by post.

I loved the course from Day 1. I immersed myself in it as in a warm bath. I studied Genesis, Paul and – my favourite, rather to my own surprise – the Cistercians in England in the twelfth century. And among those Cistercians I discovered and fell in love with, as it were, Aelred of Rievaulx. I had been to Rievaulx Abbey, and I visited it again after finishing the course. It is wonderfully atmospheric, in spite of all the bossy English Heritage notices. If you arrive late and out of season, when the sun is going down, you really can get some sense of what life was like in this bowl of the Yorkshire Dales, where sheep bleat through the soft air and the light gleams through the majestic ruins, archways, slit windows, whole 'rooms' and magnificent spaces.

I came to love Aelred because I came to know him. So much of that time is very distant and different, yet there is enough left of Aelred's writings, we know so much of his life and personality, that he can come closer to us than many who have lived later. Or so we suppose. Life then was not like life now and it is easy to fall into the error of familiarity. But human is human. Aelred was a great and good man.

This evening, with the rain setting in early, I take down several books about the Cistercians and about Aelred, marvelling in particular at how often and how far he travelled, on horseback, to meetings every three years of all the Cistercian abbots in Rome. Rome seems far enough if you drive there today. The journey from

Yorkshire would have taken months, was perilous and must certainly have been wearying. Aelred was a good administrator. He loved and also looked after his monks at Rievaulx, made plans for improvements to the abbey, took charge of the outlying tenant farms and of the lay brothers who worked in them, beyond the monastery itself. He was well read, devout, perspicacious, and he knew the world – as a young man he had been a steward in the court of the King of Scotland and it was in King David's company that he was travelling down through northern England when the little band sought and naturally were given hospitality at Rievaulx. Aelred fell in love with the place, and he felt an overwhelming call to become a monk there. He rode away that time – but he was soon back, looking down from the hill above on the calm, handsome, grey stone buildings, certain then that he must stay. And stay he did, eventually to become abbot, to write, preach, study, work, organise, pray. He was as devout a man as could be found – when not all those who became monks were, or took the monastic life seriously and lived it so well.

As a result of taking cold baths – and baths in North Yorkshire water come down from the hills above would have been icy – in order to curb his strong physical desires and do penance, he became arthritic and was in extreme pain for much of his later life. The pain of arthritis is severe enough now, with analgesics as strong as can be. I looked at the book in my hand, and at a page in which the scribe tells how much physical agony the Abbot of Rievaulx was constantly in, and I imagined what it would have been like in the fierce Yorkshire winters, when ice and snow lasted for months and the great fires that blazed inside the walls would barely have taken the chill off the smallest spaces.

Aelred was a good man and a good monk and a good abbot

simply because he believed that love and friendship were every-thing. For him, the monastery should be a community of friends. The monastic life was about friendship.

Perhaps that is why, from so far away, he speaks so clearly and readily to us now.

I had thought of doing a PhD about Aelred of Rievaulx. But I was put off, by myself and others, for all the right reasons. I could easily have become one of those people who never quite manages to finish their thesis but I might also, in stumbling along with it, have failed to write the books it is more important for me to write. So I just read his work and about his life and about twelfth-cen-tury Cistercian monasticism, from time to time, as tonight, and sometimes go back to Rievaulx, which, thank God, is still there, even as a ruin. Plenty of monasteries, destroyed by that vandal Henry VIII, were razed to the ground, with perhaps a few bases of stone pillars left, like stumps of teeth. I am glad there is so much left of Rievaulx. When you stand alone there, even though the sky and not a roof is over your head, you can hear the whispers of monastic chant and the faint ghostly swish of the heavy robes, see the shadowy procession of hooded figures on their way to and from the chapel. And there is nothing remotely spooky about it.

I sometimes read a chapter or so of one of the histories I studied while doing my MA – books by Dom David Knowles or, more recently, Janet Burton – and I dive back into those times with joy. But I was right not to attempt a PhD. I am not scholarly material. Keeping up the subject, and Biblical studies, via 'books about' is the most I will ever do.

One of my modules, about St Paul, was tough, because there is a whole new school of thought about him, about his Jewishness, and I did not fully understand it. Whether you are a believer or not is irrelevant to the study of Paul's life. Jerome Murphy-O'Connor has written two biographies which seem to get right under his skin, and they follow him on his physical as well as his spiritual journeys, taking us with him as willing companions. Like Aelred and his fellow abbots, Paul travelled hundreds of miles, some-times by ship – and suffered after being shipwrecked, too – but mainly on foot. Travel was even more dangerous then and people banded together for safety against marauding wild animals and brigands. Paul went to and from his churches all over the Holy Land, numerous times. He does not strike one as an especially 'nice' man, he was fierce and neither relaxed nor amiable, but he loved his disciples in a stern sort of way, he worked hard as a tent-maker, he stumped through heat and dust over hard terrain in the course of being a follower of Christ – and, like so many, was eventually imprisoned and executed for his pains. They were made of strong stuff, men like Paul and Aelred.

SOMEONE SOMEWHERE COMPLAINED recently that there were far too many books 'about books and reading'. Meta-literature is probably what it is called and when I see such a book, I generally buy it. I see I have on one shelf: *The Yellow-Lighted Bookshop*, *Ex Libris*, *The Child that Books Built*, *The Bookshop Book*, *The Library Book*, *100 Books You Must Read Before You Die*, *Where I'm Reading From*, *A History of Reading*, *So Many Books, So Little Time*, *The Library at Night*, *A Reader on Reading*, *The Pleasures of Reading in an Age of Distraction*, *Women Who Read are Dangerous*, *Phantoms on the Bookshelves*, *How Literature Saved My Life*. The last is by an

American author, David Shields, and he has some good things to say, but he is also a 'the novel is dead' person and if anything ever flew in the face of the evidence, that does. If the novel is dead, what are all those people who write them doing? Why the queues for creative writing degrees? Why so many novels published? Why so many printed and sold in bookshops? Why so many now self-published as e-books by novelists whose work never sees the light of physical print but who still manage to make money out of them? Quality is not the point here. It is a question of numbers. Novels are written and published in their many thousands because they are read ditto. Or else they would not be. Shields says, rather sadly it seems, that 'the novel has long been dead to me'.

Meanwhile, in the pomposity department, he files a nice story. There is a very prestigious American prize called the National Book Award. In 1987, 'after the fiction panel did not name Toni Morrison the winner, she approached the committee's chair … and said, "Thank you for ruining my life." If your life depends on winning an award chosen by a few people over lunch, there's something wrong with your life.'

There is something wrong with the lives of other writers, too, judging by the story about the one whose editor was driving him somewhere when they heard the announcement of the Man Booker shortlist on the radio. The author was so disappointed, shocked and angry that he was not included that the car had to be stopped while he beat his fists on the dashboard and screamed at his editor. I knew a then-famous novelist who did not/could not/would not speak to anyone for twenty-four hours, so astonished and furious was he that his latest book was not the American Book of the Month Club Choice. And I learned quite a bit about people's sense of entitlement when I was a judge of the Man Booker Prize myself. At one of those terrible prize-giving dinners, when the announcement of the winning book was named, yet another anonymous author banged something again – the table this time – and said, 'I have been cheated of this prize.' Disappointment is entirely understandable. If your name is mentioned promisingly in conjunction with a valuable prize, or you are even shortlisted, you are entitled to feel disappointed when you do not win. But that's it. Otherwise, 'Get a life' really is the appropriate response.

———————•O•———————

A LONG SKEIN of pink-footed geese has just gone over towards the marshes.

———————•O•———————

THIS GOLDEN OCTOBER continues to drift slowly down like a twirling leaf. Sitting in the garden in the sun reading a biography of Jean Rhys.

Two young muntjac deer come for the windfall apples at the far end of the meadow. Indeed, not only for the windfalls … they reach up and take the apples right off the branches. Sometimes, they play, chasing one another in and out of the trees. Pretty things, but a worry on the roads. One jumped out of the hedge, followed by two young, when I was driving the leafy back road to Holt and I barely missed them. Yet I have never seen a single badger in Norfolk, alive or dead. Our Cotswold fields were riddled with badger setts. You could hear them lumbering about at night, they attacked the Border terriers and the road kill was significant.

Still reading the Jean Rhys biography. I have re-read all her novels during the last eighteen months. I muddle them up, apart from *Wide Sargasso Sea*, which is her masterpiece and will surely remain as one of best novels of the twentieth century – and it does not seem to detract from my understanding and admiration of it that I have never read *Jane Eyre*.

I was accused of setting my face against doing so recently, and maybe that has become true, but at least when people find echoes of it all over *The Woman in Black*, I know they are wrong. Or do I? Can a book have echoes of another book which the author has never read? I feel I have read *JE*, I know so much about it – the mad wife in the attic, the blindness … But that's the sum of what Jean Rhys does, too. But although the biography is interesting, and beyond poignant, and although Jean was a strange mixture – a genius and a monster; a pathetic, lonely woman stuck, in her last years, in a damp, ugly modern house in a remote Devon village she hated – I think the puzzle is easy enough to solve. Not only the careful biography, but the chapter about her in *Difficult Women* written in the 1970s by David Plante, give the clues and the answer. Everything that was wrong with her, all of her dreadful behaviour, her melancholy, her aggressive moods, her impulsiveness, her maudlin outbursts, her inability to write other than slowly, painfully and in a muddle – all can be laid at the feet of alcohol. Jean Rhys succumbed to drink early and she was a hopeless alcoholic the whole of her adult life. It is astonishing that it did not kill her years earlier. She must have had an extraordinarily strong constitution. But it destroyed her mentally. There is nothing more pathetic, and tedious, than the rantings of a drinker. The friends who stood by her and put up with her abuse and ingratitude were saints.

And now none of it matters, not in the slightest. Out of a wreck of a life, out of disastrous relationships, out of misery and loneliness and error, she wrote great novels, a distillation of her own life and psyche – for she was another who could never invent. Everything of her is in the books, everything is about her in some way. Isn't that all we need to know?

What she is about – other than exploited women and women who are their own worst enemies – is style, in the way Muriel Spark is about style. They are both dangerous to other writers, in that you need to beware reading their books if you are mid-book yourself. They have a style and a manner which is extremely infectious. I don't think I have ever 'caught' another writer's characters, or scenes or atmosphere, let alone their plots, aka stories, but I have caught style many a time until I realised what I was doing and pulled myself up short. I certainly caught Muriel Spark. I almost caught Ivy Compton-Burnett, but that's an easy one to avoid. Is she unreadable now? Was she ever 'readable'? Yet in Mona Simpson's excellent and revealing series of interviews in the *Paris Review*, Hilary Mantel says she re-reads ICB often, in order to remind herself of what fine writing is, and I yield to no one in my admiration of Hilary. I don't think I agree with her on this, though – or maybe it's the old 'Marmite' thing.

HM also says that she very often re-reads Robert Louis Stevenson's *Kidnapped*, because it is the perfect book. He is certainly the perfect writer. When I went back to *Dr Jekyll and Mr Hyde* recently, my toes curled up with delight, not so much in the story – though that is gripping enough – but in the writing, the style, the shaping of the book, the narrative line and voice … all of that. If ever a creative writing course insists on certain books being read by the students before pen is lifted, those books should include *Kidnapped* and *Dr Jeykll*. But I don't suppose reading anything is obligatory for those courses, which are as thick as autumn leaves on the ground. Writing is the thing. Ye gods.

———————●•O•●————————

A FEW MONTHS AGO some scientists from University College London were here. UCL runs an aquatic life and conservation MA course and has linked up with the local people who are responsible for the river Glaven eel project.

And it was discovered that we have eels in our pond. Nets were put out one day and inspected the next and there were sixteen eels of various sizes, which was, apparently, a Good Thing, the cause of much rejoicing. I could not see it, especially on finding out that eels migrate and that they may slither about darkly through our long grass at any time.

Now the scientists have been back, setting their nets again – this time in the company of about fifteen graduate students. Sadly, the nets were empty. Not an eel. Where have they gone? I can't say I was interested or cared much, though I used to be rather partial to smoked eel. But then I listened to some of their scientific talk, having been about as uninterested in those dark slithering things as it is possible to be, and after I had listened I bought *The Book of Eels* by Tom Fort. One book leads to another is the rule of life, and this led me back to Samuel Taylor Coleridge's *The Rhyme of the Ancient Mariner*:

Beyond the shadow of the ship
I watched the water-snakes:
They moved in tracks of shining white

And when they reared, the elfish light
Fell off in hoary flakes.

Those were eels. I learned that they start to become silver-white and phosphorescent while they are leaving our pond for the nearby river, and thence on to other rivers and the sea until … until they reach the Sargasso Sea. No, really. The Wide Sargasso Sea. There they spawn, three miles down. Then the older eels die while the young begin the perilous journey back to our rivers, and possibly even my own pond. It takes them up to three years.

And I thought they were just nasty black slimy things that were here one day, gone the next.

People have been fascinated by eels for thousands of years, I read, but it was only in the 1970s that someone actually discovered the facts about their life cycle. I suppose one day they will tag an eel from here and trawl the Sargasso Sea for it years later.

———•○•———

THE BARN OWL has not been around here for a few days. The man cut the meadow for the last time this summer, so perhaps the naked grass means that four-legged owl food has run away. Earlier in the year, when the owl man came to look in our boxes, he did not find any young owls, as he has done in the last two, but in a nearby field he found three babies in a hollow tree. He ringed them, as usual. The one we like to call 'our' barn owl, and who often sits on the posts, or even on the washing-line prop morning and evening, often for weeks on end, was ringed by him when a few weeks old. So I reckon we have owl rights. They are such extraordinary creatures, not white in spite of their ghostliness, but a creamy honey colour, darker on top of their wings. Their absolute silence when in flight, the way their heads swivel, the looks they give you – what birds! They are haughty, supercilious, proud.

Lila was only two and visiting once when the owl man appeared to do his ringing. He brought a white cotton drawstring bag, and came right to the house, by the back door, so that we could all watch. My grand-daughter stared in amazement, her eyes really like saucers, as he drew out the young owl from the bag, inspected it, let it open its wings to their full extent – which even on a baby owl is pretty wide – and then ringed it without any fuss, folded its wings gently together and slipped it back in the cotton bag. Two and a half years later and she still remembers.

It is a joy that she is now having read to her some of the stories we read to her mother, and often from the very same copies. The most recent favourite is *Tales of Polly and the Hungry Wolf* by Catherine Storr, which was loved by us all thirty-five years ago. Lila's father does a very impressive wolf's voice. And so the same stories are re-born over and over again. *The Elephant and the Bad Baby*, *Stanley & Rhoda, Each Peach Pear Plum, Burglar Bill, Mog the Forgetful Cat, The Tiger Who Came to Tea* and so on, to *My Naughty Little Sister*, that everlasting favourite, and now, to my delight, *The Magic Faraway Tree*.

The authors get no more money from having precious family copies passed down the generations, but the pleasure in immortality must outweigh that deprivation. Well, almost.

———◆◉◆———

'I HATE HALLOWEEN', someone wrote on my Facebook page, and I do sympathise. Like so many other things in life, Halloween is not what it was, it is far worse, and involves massive retail sales of horrible masks and black rubber bats, and teenagers banned from buying flour in supermarkets. Bonfire Night was the big thing when I was a child. Mischief Night, as we called Hallowe'en in Yorkshire, was a very minimal affair.

It is also the season when any theatre playing *The Woman in Black* is packed, of course, And this is also when questions from students and teachers pour in on a daily basis.

It has been a set text in schools for many years now and I answer the same questions annually. Some are easy. Some less so. Some impossible and those are the intriguing ones, when I feel I need to have the students in front of me – and the teachers too, for that matter– in order to try and help them understand. But I don't do school visits any more. I am too old and too busy writing other books to go up and down the country.

The thing they do not quite get – and why would they, we all have to come to it for the first time – is that the book stands by itself. In a sense, the author is irrelevant. Certainly, the author does not have all the correct answers, as if this were a maths exam. Teaching that the text stands alone is really teaching deconstructionism and an awful lot of high-flown nonsense got sucked into that original, rather clear idea. The other problem is that I tend to be shadowy and vague when it comes to certain things in novels and the precise date when they are set is the first. My editor always calls the period in which I set some books 'Hill Time'. *Strange Meeting*, being about the First World War, is easy. But I suppose the main events of *The Woman in Black* must happen somewhere between 1918 and 1929. Or perhaps between 1900 and 1914? I actually do not know. And I wonder how much it matters. But they are very persistent. They need chapter and verse.

I suppose it is both obvious and disappointing to young readers to point out that this is a story, an invention. That none of it actually happened. That these characters do not and never did and never will exist. I made them up. Because they want to know about things that are outside of the book, in another part of those characters' lives, about which I have not written, and know nothing. 'What happened to Kipps after his wife died?' 'Why didn't Jennet kill her sister's child and no other?' 'Why did she allow her child to be taken out in a pony and trap with just the nanny? (He probably wasn't even wearing a seat belt)?' I do not know the answer to any of these questions, and I feel I am chickening out when I say so, but if they are to understand anything about fiction/stories/ novels/literature and how they work, they have to grasp this. It seems obvious to me, but I have been reading and writing books for over fifty years and I have a degree in English. They are just beginning. I must remember that.

The favourite question, of course, is, 'Where did you get your inspiration from?'

I flounder. I waffle about the ingredients of the classic English ghost story when really I ought to just say 'God' and leave it at that.

———•O•———

I WAS REMEMBERING TODAY how Stephen Mallatratt (who adapted the book as a stage play) and I used to laugh about it. We laughed out of surprise and a sense of the unlikely. We laughed out of pleasure and amazement and sheer disbelief.

We had expected the play to run for six weeks in Scarborough, over Christmas. When it eventually opened in the West End, the laughing started, and it went on. Stephen kept all the stats – how many performances, how much money – and would ring me up a couple of times a year to give them to me. Then the incredulous laughter would begin. When it opened in Mexico City, we laughed more. When it did five years there, we were hysterical. Japan … Australia … Broadway … We were aching. It did very well in Japan, which has a long tradition of ghost stories in their culture. On Broadway it bombed. Twice. And Germany. The Germans just don't get it, but the Scandinavians do. The French don't. India does. And so on. When ticket sales were rocky for a time, we sobered up a bit, but then, as well as playing in London, it started touring the UK, which had us on the floor. I so remember that laughter. I doubt I have ever laughed so much.

And then Stephen died.

There has never been anyone else to laugh with about how unlikely it has been in quite that way.

———————•○•———————

'WHEN THE TIDE IS SHOWN at 9 on the table, it will generally overtop the car park.'

The car park goes by a better local name – the Carnser. The Norfolk word for a heron is a Harnser, hence …

It overtopped the car park and the road and almost went up the hotel drive. I had not checked before I drove down through Blakeney, where men were rescuing boats that bobbed about in the middle of the road, and not a centimetre of car park visible. That only happens a few times a year and, so long as it is not any worse, it is always worth a look. The tide was just on the turn and draining away rapidly, the water silvery and slippery as fish, and a few people even crabbing where the cars ought to be. Blakeney crab, reared on bacon. There was a brisk breeze and big moon through last night, which helped to swell the tide.

There are probably whole libraries full of books on the subject, but I read a new one recently: *Tide: The Science and Lore of the Greatest Force on Earth* by Hugh Aldersey-Williams, which was fascinating and very informative for anyone interested in tides in general and those on the North Norfolk coast in particular. The author spent twenty-four hours alone on Blakeney Point while two tides came and went, and his almost minute-by-minute record of even the tiniest things he observed makes awesome reading – so awesome I am tempted to follow in his footsteps. Just not quite tempted enough.

Living by the North Sea again, after having been born and spent the first sixteen years of my life beside it, I feel that tides have been in my blood and bones from the beginning. The link never leaves one. The most astonishing thing of all is that you can buy booklets of the tides tables for a whole year ahead and, indeed, I think they are mathematically predictable for much longer – probably until the end of time, other things being equal. A surge, such as the dangerous and terrifying one we had here four years ago, is never predictable though. Other factors – wind strength and direction, the phase of the moon, and so on – all have to combine to make the perfect storm.

This morning's high water was a baby by comparison.

———•◦•———

THE TREES HAVEN'T TURNED PROPERLY yet, there is just the

flick of a yellow brush stroke here and there. Until there is a frost, there will be no New England scarlet and gold.

One of those days when there is nothing I want to read. Everything I pick up is wrong. Old favourites. Meh. New titles. Meh. There has to be something.

And then, lo! This week's *Grazia* magazine is here and, what do you know, it is all about the Kardashians.

━━●○●━━

ALMOST EVERY WRITER I have known or read on the subject of being a writer says that they had a childhood full of books, and that if they were lonely, sad, cross or in trouble, they always turned to a book, often a much-loved one. They found consolation, companionship, solace, escape, excitement and inspiration in books, they spent as much free time as they could in libraries, had special reading places – often hidden ones, where they could not be found or interrupted. It was either that, or the old standby, under the bedclothes with a torch. Books did something for them which nothing else could do, not family, siblings, friends, games, the movies, television …

A young friend of mine came visiting when she was about nine and, as usual, went to the bookshelves, found what she fancied reading and settled herself on the kitchen sofa. There was not a squeak out of her, also as usual, but when I went in there, she said, 'Don't you think it is very strange?'

I looked over. She was holding her book up.

'The cover's quite nice but otherwise it doesn't look very interesting, does it? I mean, if you came from Mars and had never seen a book, you wouldn't get excited by this, would you? Not like you might over toys. It's just a lump of paper covered in card and, if you open it, it's all the same. Black marks on every white sheet. If it didn't have a picture on the front you wouldn't look at it again, would you?'

I agreed.

'*But,*' she said, 'just think … Inside this there is a whole world, a whole lot of people, a whole lot of things happening, a whole lot of places you want to go to and … well, there's all that. And if I hold it upside down all those things somehow fall out of it. Do you see what I mean?'

———•○•———

THE OLD ADVICE about not buying a book for its cover is no longer good. I have often done so and rarely regretted it, because cover design has improved by miles in the last decades. I have sometimes not bought a book because of its title, though, and even more because of the blurb. Blurb writing is one of the most difficult of all book skills. It has to give the flavour of a book, address the exact audience which would most appreciate it while not alienating the others, synopsise without giving too much away – especially not a surprise ending – explain the book, refer to its author's previous work … Entice, excite … All within 150 words or less.

So it is not surprising that sometimes blurbs get it wrong. I was put off by both the title and the blurb of Zadie Smith's novel *On Beauty*. 'On' anything sounds like a nineteenth-century essay by William Hazlitt, preachy, dull, without human reference. The blurb explains that the author was paying homage to E. M. Forster's *Howards End* (the hero of *On Beauty* is called Howard) and that it is about two rival academics who have both written books about Rembrandt. Together with the mention of hip-hop and teenage American rappers, it did not seem like my sort of novel. I would not like to have been given the job of writing the blurb for *On Beauty* myself, mind, trying to gather all the multifarious threads together into a crisp outline, leaving out nothing important.

Anyway, I ought to know better by now. I have enjoyed many a novel by simply picking it up and starting to read it from Chapter One, Page One, Line One, deliberately avoiding any blurbs, introductions or descriptions, on front cover or back. I should have done the same with this.

Yes, it is indeed about rival academics writing about Rembrandt, and their teenager kids engaged in popular culture. It is about American families and multi-culturalism ... In fact, if I think about it, I still do not care about the subject matter – there is so much in it that I would never knowingly read about. Yet I discovered that it is a rich, dense book, that it rings true, that these people are real people, known and understood through and through, though sometimes alien. That it is witty and wonderfully well written, intelligent and learned, even if some of the cultural lessons come across as lectures. Doesn't matter. No fine novel is flawless. Look at Dickens. It is some feat to write a novel about people of the sort in whom I am uninterested, set in a country to which I have never been and feel no affinity with, about a subject that I find tedious ... and have me engaged from the first, absorbed in the whole, looking forward to reading the next slab.

On Beauty is also a campus novel. Malcolm Bradbury, Mary McCarthy, David Lodge, Kingsley Amis, Alison Lurie ... all have written telling, involved, disturbingly accurate examples, and now Smith jumps in, with wit and a bullshit-ometer like a precision tool. Her observations are spot on – as they would be, given that she is now an academic herself, in America. Having been married to a university professor for four decades plus, I can vouch for the accuracy of the internecine squabbles, not to mention rivalry, showmanship and one-upmanship. But recording conversations and repeating them on the page is easy. Digging below the skin and the voice timbre to the person beneath is only easy to get wrong.

Zadie Smith has that thing without which all writers ultimately fail – an ear for how people speak, what they say as against what they really mean, their intonation, the smallest shades of difference between speakers that indicates education, class, age, intelligence, social adeptness. She also has an eye for detail which, though not always quite as important, makes fiction live.

There is little doubt that she has her own measure, knows her own worth and always has. She is secure in her writer's skin and you cannot buy that sort of confidence.

I have now to read her last two novels – I read her first, *White Teeth*, when it came out in 1999. I do not know anything about the others, being someone who rarely reads the book review pages of newspapers, so I can start at Chapter One, Page One, Line One and wait to be surprised. Without reading the blurbs.

———•○•———

A FEW DECADES AGO the *Times Literary Supplement* asked prominent literary people for their favourite out-of-print authors and two, Philip Larkin and Lord David Cecil, chose Barbara Pym. Not many people had heard of her then, but a new season of admiration and sales for her books was kicked off and it was especially tool. Her observations are spot on – as they would be, given that she is now an academic herself, in America. Having been married to a university professor for four decades plus, I can vouch for the accuracy of the internecine squabbles, not to mention rivalry, showmanship and one-upmanship. But recording conversations and repeating them on the page is easy. Digging below the skin and the voice timbre to the person beneath is only easy to get wrong.

Zadie Smith has that thing without which all writers ultimately fail – an ear for how people speak, what they say as against what they really mean, their intonation, the smallest shades of difference between speakers that indicates education, class, age, intelligence, social adeptness. She also has an eye for detail which, though not always quite as important, makes fiction live.

There is little doubt that she has her own measure, knows her own worth and always has. She is secure in her writer's skin and you cannot buy that sort of confidence.

I have now to read her last two novels – I read her first, *White Teeth*, when it came out in 1999. I do not know anything about the others, being someone who rarely reads the book review pages of newspapers, so I can start at Chapter One, Page One, Line One and wait to be surprised. Without reading the blurbs.

———•○•———

A FEW DECADES AGO the *Times Literary Supplement* asked prominent literary people for their favourite out-of-print authors and two, Philip Larkin and Lord David Cecil, chose Barbara Pym. Not many people had heard of her then, but a new season of admiration and sales for her books was kicked off and it was especially nice that she was still alive to enjoy the fuss – it's usually too late. (Pym died of cancer a few years later.)

I read most of the re-issued novels at the time and never entirely saw the point of the praise, probably because everyone compared them to Jane Austen and that is never a good recommendation to me. I forgot them, more or less, until I saw a mention of *Quartet in Autumn* in Shirley Hazzard's essays and reviews, and that *is* a recommendation.

Hazzard reviewed her alongside Muriel Spark and the latter comes off by far the best, but still she says that what Barbara Pym does on a small canvas she nevertheless does supremely well.

Quartet in Autumn is a perceptive and touching novel, about two men and two women who all work in the same office – of what sort of firm we are never told, and it matters little because their work is both routine and dull and of no interest either to them or to us. The book is set in the 1950s, but it might have been in the 1920s because women of thirty-five are seen as middle aged, and fifty-five positively ancient. Men of forty-five are well past their prime and looking ahead to retirement. They all are, and soon retirement comes. They are all single, live alone in grim bedsitters, bleak flats, a house left by an aunt. They have few friends, though one man spends his life going to church – or rather, churches, for he is familiar with a whole host of them and does the rounds. They eat sad little lunches by themselves in cafés and even sadder poached eggs on toast or tinned pilchards at home every evening. One of the women is decidedly eccentric and gets worse in the course of the book, dressing like a bag lady and collecting empty milk bottles and stashing them away by the dozen in her shed.

Even friendship, in these novels, is hesitant and ringed about with embarrassment.

I won't return to the others, but I am keeping *Quartet in Autumn* on the shelf and I would recommend it – not lightly, though. It isn't a novel for everyone.

———•◦•———

HAD TO STOP THE CAR along the coast road just beyond Salthouse, beside the stream and a great reed bed, because the boot was not properly closed. As I reached up for the handle something caught my eye. It was a bittern, moving out of and back into the reeds. I have never seen one before, probably never will again. It was unmistakeable. It had that ugly, paleolithic look of herons and egrets, to whom bitterns are related. All I have to do now is hear one boom. These things always happen by chance, at least where I am concerned, though the dedicated birders and twitchers put in the hours and are (sometimes) rewarded.

———•◦•———

A FRIEND INTRODUCED ME to the novels of the American writer Richard Ford. I had never heard of him, but I am not ashamed of that. We all have massive gaps in our reading. Which is good, we need gaps – for the pleasure of filling them.

I like long novels which suck me into the everyday life of provincial America, so that I find out what people eat and what furniture they have in their houses, how they celebrate birthdays and Christmas and relate, or don't, to their next-door neighbours, how their communities work, how far they travel, what size the schools are and how their teachers teach and their pastors preach. Above all,

I like to get inside their heads. That is why I found Ford's *The Sportswriter* so interesting. The narrator, Frank Bascombe, has been a sportswriter on a newspaper. He has also been married and lost a son, whose death tore the marriage apart. Americans write well about family – usually broken and dispersed. They write about it better than we do now, though not better than the Victorians. Bascombe's wife, referred to always as X, has moved out, leaving him in the family home with a rather off-screen lodger. He also has a girlfriend, a nurse who hails from Texas, and perhaps Bascombe, or the reader, will decide that she isn't right/good enough for him. But she is the one who decides that, when she announces round her family's dinner table that they don't have much in common and that she doesn't love him enough to marry him.

He also belongs to a marvellous invention of Ford's – the local Divorced Men's Club. It doesn't dive very deep. The husbands are drinking buddies and fishing pals more than anything more complex. Complexity only surfaces, to Bascombe's discomfiture, when one of them commits suicide. Nothing is safe, nothing is easy-going, nothing is allowed to jog along in the shallows of small town life.

So, there I was, grateful for having discovered Richard Ford and *The Sportswriter*, admiring it a great deal, looking forward to the later Bascombe novels – three more. And then, in search of a reference for something else, I came upon a piece by *Vanity Fair* writer James Wolcott about *The Sportswriter*. When I had finished it, I wondered if he and I had read the same novel. This sometimes happens, especially if you read book reviews regularly. It is one just one of the reasons why I don't.

Wolcott finds the novel full of condescension and bookish

banality. 'Frank Bascombe isn't a decent man, he's a long-faced creep pulling the long face of a decent man. It's a pious impersonation that fooled the critics ...' and so on and so sneeringly on. Clever criticism? Too clever by half. But whatever Wolcott or any other critic may say, whatever agenda they may have, whatever axe to grind – and believe me, there usually is one – I found *The Sportswriter* a deeply satisfying book and, more than anything else, I found it a very *genuine* novel. Which is quite the opposite of the phoney one Wolcott seems to have found.

——•○•——

WHY SHIRLEY HAZZARD'S book of essays, *We Need Silence to Find Out What We Think*, is not published in the UK, I do not know, but perhaps now that she has died and so is being re-discovered and praised all round, someone will have the good sense to pick it up. I have a very physical relationship with my books, which is probably only one reason why I never got on with an e-reader. I write in the margins, dog-ear the pages, underline whole sentences, but I have not treated a book so intimately for years as I have manhandled these essays. There is something memorable, some insight or wise deduction, some wonderfully expressed observation, something witty, pithy or beautiful, on almost every page.

> But art is not technology and cannot be 'mastered'. It is an endless access to revelatory states of mind, a vast extension of living experience and a way of communing with the dead. An intimacy with truth, through which, however much instruction is provided and absorbed, each of us must pass alone.

She herself must have left her physical mark on books. Either that or she had a phenomenal memory. She quotes from all manner of writers – on just one page there is Samuel Johnson, Lord Byron and Eugenio Montale, Giacomo Leopardi, W. H. Auden and Cleanth Brooks. Not that she does not have a mind and opinions of her own. She does and they are expressed clearly and elegantly.

The more I read, the more I am sure that above everything it is the quality of the writing that counts. How often do I start a promising-looking novel, with a beautiful or dramatic setting, intriguing subject matter, good, well-created structure, only to abandon it after a few chapters, or even pages, because the writing is bad – bad or boring, dull, clumsy writing, without distinctiveness, without individuality, form, balance, harmony, tone. Not fancy writing, not pretentious writing, not innovative – in the worst sense – writing. Just bad writing. It will not do. Of course, fine words are not all and we should forgive the occasional ill-formed sentence, or banal paragraph – but only that. Graceful, elegant, apposite, balanced, intelligent prose is then good, is beautiful prose and fit for purpose. Some writers could make a book about bathroom fittings delightful and satisfying to read. Shirley Hazzard is such a one.

I WAS LOOKING for something on Amazon, and slid sideways, as you do. There was a section of titles which had been shortlisted for various prizes over the last year or two. I looked carefully at the novel category in each – say, twenty-five titles, and, apart from the winners in each one, I did not recognise any of them, they had sunk without trace. I could not even remember having heard of them at all. Some of the winners have not fared much better either, yet people still go on believing that their book will break through. People still want to be writers. People dream of giving up the day job. If you asked any one of these aspirants how they would feel if their novel was long- or even shortlisted for the Costa/Baileys/Desmond Elliott, let alone the Man Booker, they would doubtless say their dreams had come true, they had made it, reached the peak of their ambition, that from now on the writing life was a primrose path. I wouldn't draw their attention to those lists of the so-recently forgotten. Robert Robinson used to entertain panellists on his radio and TV programmes, during the warm-up or the inevitable technical hitch, by reciting a list of names and then asking you what they had in common. They were all winners of the Nobel Prize for Literature and none were familiar. Obscurity had shrouded ever single one.

IT HAS RAINED ALL DAY and, as usual, the lanes are awash, with massive floods across the road to Wiveton. You would think it had been pouring for a month.

NOVEMBER

'FOR ALL THE SAINTS.' One of the best hymn tunes. As with the Bible and the Book of Common Prayer, you do not have to be a Christian, or even a believer, to appreciate and be uplifted by hearing a church full of people singing something out of *Hymns Ancient & Modern*. Modern hymns are awful. I don't know why they bothered. If they felt the words were outdated, and so of limited appeal to the young, it would not have been beyond the wit of an Anglican subcommittee to write new ones to the old tunes. But no, baby went out with the bathwater and we got slush and soup and sentimentality.

NOTEBOOKS. I start to use them, lose them, never fill one because I have started another and so they pile up, all shapes and sizes, with two or twenty-two pages covered in scribble and oddments. This is shameful when I think back to our first exercise books at school and how we had to turn them over and write on top of the lines already used, because there was still a paper shortage after the war. After that, if new ones still had not come in, we had to write long-ways, in the margin. Now, paper is cheap and I buy a notebook when I see one.

Flipping through a few just now, looking for a half-remembered line I shall probably never find, I do find this: 'It is true enough, writers all do use each other.' Is it true, and if so, in what sense? Yes, as a writer I 'use', albeit unconsciously, most of the books I have ever read. It is not a question of plagiarism. But the atmosphere of a novel can linger in the mind for half a century and then one finds oneself re-creating it. I did that with Dickens and *Printer's Devil Court*, with Virginia Woolf and *Air and Angels* – though there it is the style. Other novels may make one rush off and start a novel of one's own, which is totally different. Sometimes just the mention of a book in a trade journal will kick-start something. I think of it as the interweaving of literature down the centuries, not as any sort of personal failure. What is poor form is when a book is a bestseller, and half a dozen other publishers immediately look for a manuscript like it – they even echo it on their own cover, with font and image, to make the reader pick it up because of the subliminal association.

RAINING. Sky like the inside of a saucepan. I have just received the proofs of *From the Heart*. Now it is in proper print, I shall be able to read it and see what it is like. I can't judge on typescript. I have read many others say the same. I suppose it is a question of distancing it from oneself, the writer. That and time.

THERE IS A SHORTHAND, shared among people who have read the same book more than once, and mostly they are parents. Once learned, the words of the stories stay with you for a lifetime. In the doctor's surgery, I sat near a mother reading to her 3-year-old.

'So Chicken Licken, Henny Penny, Cocky Locky and Drakey Lakey, scurried off to tell the King that the sky was falling in.'

She turned the page.

'You've missed out Ducky Lucky,' I said, beating the 3-year-old to it by a nanosecond.

A FRIEND MADE A COMMENT on Facebook about someone's new dog. 'It looks like Bottomley Potts,' she said.

'All covered in spots,' someone chimed in at once.

Someone else contributed 'Hercules Morse …'

'As big as a horse …'

We had finished the entire book in the time it takes to drink your morning coffee. (Facebook being the solitary writer's social break in the middle of work.) How many people know *Hairy Maclary from Donaldson's Dairy* as well as our little gang?

The only other children's book I have found recalled by heart so widely among adults is Janet and Allan Ahlbergs' *Each Peach Pear Plum*. Now there's a meta-book if ever there was one.

'SO WE BEAT ON, boats against the current, borne back ceaselessly into the past.'

The last lines of *The Great Gatsby* may be the best known – and the best – of any in fiction. First lines are always arresting, but this beautiful sentence, bringing the novel to a dying-fall conclusion, somehow seals the whole book in a bubble in one's memory. No wonder F. Scott Fitzgerald chose to have it engraved on his headstone. (Or did he choose himself?)

There are plenty of other endings which sum up the whole Sturm und Drang of a mighty novel and bring it to rest.

'I lingered round them, under that benign sky; watched the moths fluttering among the heath and hare-bells; listened to the soft wind breathing through the grass; and wondered how anyone could ever imagine unquiet slumbers for the sleepers in that quiet earth.' *Wuthering Heights*, another book full of huge emotions, like storms at sea, brought to such a peaceful close.

I wish I had written either of those.

Meanwhile, it has rained the entire day and I have not accomplished very much.

IN THE END, you just don't get on with some writers, it's a pure case of Dr Fell, but I have been thinking that, regarding my long-term inability to get on with Patricia Highsmith, there has to be more to it than that. *Beautiful Shadow*, Andrew Wilson's thorough and interesting biography of her, has helped, but I also have my own idea. Highsmith is not a describer. Her characters inhabit large and small, famous and unknown American cities and the suburbs of those cities, but they all feel the same. We don't know what they look like, in what way they are different from all the other cities in America. Apartment blocks, small houses in anonymous streets, walkways, train stations ... but we could be anywhere. It all feels anonymous. She is good at suspense and tension, but those are not the same as atmosphere. *The Talented Mr Ripley* is an exception. The Italian village to which Ripley comes is so well evoked we can smell it, feel the heat, see the colours. The interior of the house he rents – we could walk round it and feel at home.

But too many of the books lack a vital element because of their bareness. They have characters: we are told where they go, what they do, what they say – and that's it.

The second vacuum is a moral one. Andrew Wilson points out, and picks up on other critics who have done the same, that Highsmith has no moral compass. None. Ripley kills. Other characters kill, or commit crimes almost as bad, but there is no justice, no redemption – no comment, in fact. Does Highsmith have any desire to bring about retribution? Does she blame her characters for what they do? It seems not. She just presents these deeds and leaves them there. She herself believed life was like that. No justice and no point in any. But she is writing crime, the essential fictional mode for depicting the eternal struggle … and yet she seems not to notice either good or evil, as such. And that lack of notice leaves a blank, a vacuum, a nothing, at the heart of many of her books.

She comes out of Wilson's biography as a bit of a monster, yet she was the victim of monsters, too. Many of her relationships were death struggles between two people who could not be together because they tore one another apart – and yet who kept returning just because that tearing-apart seemed to be necessary to them. They felt only half-people without the emotional violence and conflict.

One novel of hers I read last year is very moving, though it is written in such a laconic way we do not realise that it is a domestic tragedy until many chapters in. *Edith's Diary* is a strange, disturbing, unsettling, eerie novel set in uninteresting, dull small-town America. Nothing happens. Everything happens. Life goes on and gets worse. Death happens. It is a tragedy, not a crime novel. One of those books that hangs around the corners of your mind, like cobwebs.

SEVERAL WRENS IN AND OUT of the bushes this morning, which is a welcome sight after their absence for some time. Delicate little birds. But I remember when I once examined a dead one closely, it seemed both frail and strong as wire. I think they have nested in the hedges on either side of the house. Milder winters for the last five years must be responsible, but if we have a hard one this time, they will suffer. They used to huddle together right inside a big old pile of straw and wood shavings and twigs in the old place and, so long as there are some shelters of that kind, they should be fine. Manicured gardens are a bad thing in more ways than one.

There have been morning mists, beautiful soft mounds of it lying over the water, but today there was a dense fog. Apparently, ambulances were not able to go out last night, it was so thick – visibility down to a few yards in places.

———◦———

The winter evening settles down
With smell of steaks in passageways.
Six o'clock.
The burnt-out ends of smoky days.

THAT CONJURES UP my first term at King's, and the smell of London as we came out of college on the Strand and walked down to Temple tube station. There was that river smell and a lot of boats and commercial traffic on the Thames in those days. The skyline always seemed to be scarlet in the evening.

The snatch of T. S. Eliot's *Preludes* floats about my head, as do so many snatches or poems – or indeed whole ones, learned between the ages of, I suppose, five and twenty-five. After that one stops being a sponge for verse.

I re-read poetry occasionally but very rarely anything new. I thought the other day, as I turned the page on which the week's new poem was printed in the *Spectator*, without so much as glancing at it, 'How many people who read this journal ever read the poem?' The same goes for the *New Statesman* and the *TLS*. But they go on printing them. Maybe it is out of kindness to poets. They should do a survey. There are surveys about every other bloody thing.

━━━━●•○•●━━━━

I HAVE BEEN TRYING TO DISCOVER how many novels have been published about the First World War, since I wrote *Strange Meeting* in 1971. There were very few English ones then, although Erich Maria Remarque's *All Quiet on the Western Front* was popular in translation and R. C. Sherriff's play *Journey's End* was revived from time to time. But I began working on my book in trepidation. Not only was I audacious to be attempting it at all, I was a young woman, not yet thirty. Since then, of course, there have been dozens of novels set in the period, and plenty by women.

It isn't as crowded a field as the one in which Second World War fiction resides. I have never thought of setting a novel then. I was born into that war, I still remember – just – some things about life then. It was my parents' war. They talked about it all the time, during it and forever after. 'Beforethewar' – spoken as one word – was like some sort of Garden of Eden, in which treasures were freely available, whereas sweets were rationed until my tenth birthday, in 1952.

I have no writerly feeling for the time. There are so many novels set during those years and many are, frankly, bad, and often sentimental. If I want to know what it was like, felt like, to live then, I read not only the Olivia Manning trilogies, I read Elizabeth Bowen. When I went up to King's in 1960, there were still plenty of bomb sites in London, with broken walls like teeth in a blank mouth and rosebay willowherb growing among the ruins. 'Ivy Gripped the Steps', as Bowen's short story has it. She gets the feel of wartime London better than any other novelist I know, but her style is absolutely hers, clotted and sometimes even opaque and it does not do to read her if I am writing myself. She is a fine influence in general – in her creation of places, people, situations – and wonderful on what we now call 'the built environment', but her style is hers alone, and very catching.

How do we 'catch' another writer's style? Theirs has to be distinctive to begin with. Good plain correct prose, without any individuality, the sort the best non-fiction writers employ, is exemplary and one learns from it, but that is not what I mean. Nor, really, is writing which stretches the boundaries of language, punctuation and grammar. You could not 'catch' the prose style of James Joyce by accident, yet you can, until you go back over what you have written and notice, pick up the style of Muriel Spark or William Trevor, say. I know because I have done it in both cases. Maybe creative writing courses should give their students a page or two of writers like that to read carefully and then imitate, to show how easy it is and how it ought not to be done. Ivy Compton-Burnett was a novelist about whom I was warned when I was a tyro. She wrote almost entirely in dialogue – formal, short, sharp exchanges which are the very devil to get rid of once you have started to copy them, albeit accidentally. And all this copying usually is by accident – or I hope so.

———•○•———

NOT SURE WHAT TO READ tonight. Nothing suits. I feel like a child rejecting every single sweetie in the bag. Discontented.

I have been sent a couple of proof copies of new thrillers, one by Denise Mina, one by a first-timer. I am not sure if I feel like a thriller. Do I feel like the Dickens I usually fall back on? Not really. I always used to read P. G. Wodehouse at times like this. I might get on with Book 3 of Marcel Proust's *A la recherche du temps perdu*. It has taken me five years to get this far, though. Henry James? A short story. Ah, now you're talking. But not quite. I feel like an essay and, looking through the shelves, I have found three volumes of *The Best American Essays*. Some of the American writers I least enjoy in their novels have written wonderful essays. David Foster Wallace's novels are impenetrable to me, but his essays are so intelligent, wide-ranging, crisply written – and you learn from them. Zadie Smith is one of the best essayists now writing – especially, but not only, in the field of lit crit.

And then there is James Wood, another 'best now writing', towering genius of the *New Yorker*, who has taught me more about novels, the reading and writing thereof, than anyone else since Virginia Woolf. Yes. Time for a re-read of James Wood, I think.

———•○•———

BONFIRE NIGHT SEEMS to have been three-quarters replaced by Halloween. Remembering the Yorkshire Bonfire Nights, with the obligatory treacle toffee and parkin. Do they still have that?

Halloween was Mischief Night and I was not allowed to take part. Actually, I think everyone at the convent was forbidden to have anything to do with it because it was un-Christian. I still think in essence that it is, but it is much more about fun and dressing up. Jess reports that their area of Brighton had streets full of tiny witches, ghouls and ghosties. People decorated their houses, and lit them up, everyone stayed in and the full treats buckets rapidly emptied, only to be filled up again on the other side.

But the smell of bonfires and the sparks flying upwards, and the crack and crackle and whoosh and bang takes me back in a way no Halloween ever will. The last Guy Fawkes Night I remember in Yorkshire, we had a local bonfire on the rough ground at the end of the close, and some people came, visiting relatives, who stood back in the shadows so that their faces would not be seen. I asked someone who the people were, and they asked someone else. Nobody knew, until a whisper went round that they were The Mitchells. No one believed it. But it was true. The Mitchells had won the jackpot on the Football Pools the previous month – that was £75,000, the most anyone could win – and like winning several millions on the Lottery today. They ate our parkin and drank our cocoa, standing in the dark. Everyone edged nearer and stared at them through the flame-lit darkness. They left once the fireworks were over, without speaking to anyone. In their new car.

———◦———

AFTER THE MILDEST OF OCTOBERS, we now have a cold snap. But what is cold now, after the North Yorkshire winters of my childhood?

The geese are all coming in. The hedgehog has not been seen for a week. Probably he has buried himself for his long sleep.

Time to find the best story about a long winter sleep that I have ever read, *Moominland Midwinter*, in which the Moomins close their house up bit by bit and settle down in their beds under deep soft quilts. And as they sleep, the snow comes, covering Moomin House in a soft quilt of its own. And then there is the long silence. I think this is one of the most beautiful books I know.

But what is a beautiful book? Beautifully written? Yes. But much more. Easy to suggest a frightening book. A sad book. A funny book. But a beautiful book … I go to bed, and the question haunts me before I fall asleep.

———•◦•———

I WAS REMEMBERING the library bus that used to visit our Oxfordshire village when the children were small. They loved waiting to hear the bus horn sound and then walking up the lane with their books to exchange. The children's shelves were set low and just right for them to reach. There were not many children but there was always a queue of older villagers. Detective stories. Romances. Local history. Biographies of famous politicians and military men. Cookery books. These were the most borrowed.

Thirty years later, and the children are grown women. My grand-daughter visits the library and loves not only changing and choosing her books, but going to 'visit' my books and those her mother has written. But her parents never borrow books from the library. They buy them from Amazon, or are given them. I never borrow books, either. I buy them or am sent them free by publishers, although I do browse the many charity shop book offerings regularly. There is never anything for me except the odd crime novel. The answer is not that we do not read but that we are too prosperous, although none of us are rich. Younger daughter reads avidly but I don't think she would know where her local library branch was situated – just one of the results of being a young person who works in London and rents their living space, and so is never in the same area for long enough to put down what you might call Library Roots.

We have a very good small library near here. I take them all my free copies of new titles and very pleased they are to have them. There is never a crowd in there but always a few mothers and children, and adults, too – mainly over fifty. Why not? None of this is a problem and the librarian told me recently that not one of our county libraries is under threat. Good again.

But today I heard the horn of the library bus as it parked on the corner. This is a tiny hamlet – how many people live within the sound of that horn and are at home during the day? A dozen?

I have been observing the library bus for the five years I have lived here, and I have never ever seen a single person visiting it. No mothers. No toddlers. No children. No older people. No one. It stays for thirty minutes. How much does a library bus cost to run? I have no idea. And in really remote rural corners of the county I am sure the bus is much appreciated. Used, even. But when the good local library is a mile and a half away, it is redundant. Most people have cars and there is a good bus service. If they are going to make savings, then perhaps they should make them by getting rid of the library buses which visit areas where most people have cars or can get local buses with some ease. The people who really benefit from having them are those in very remote rural corners, and whose residents are not only isolated but on low incomes, either because they are pensioners or are on basic wages. And perhaps places which are full of second/holiday homes do not need the library bus either.

I daresay I have started a hare, as usual.

———•◦•———

I OPENED THE DOOR at about ten this evening for Poppy to go out, expecting a chill blast, but it was milder. Soft air. I walked down the lane to the ford, Poppy trailing behind, to sniff every blade of grass, Orlando emerging from nowhere to accompany us. They started playing hide-and-seek, dodging in and out of the bushes and hedge. No moon. No stars. No people. The river was running gently over the stones – and the water was low. The mill at the end of the road controls the level, according to its own needs. Not many people live near a working mill that grinds the wheat into flour and bakes the bread. I always half-expect to see the Little Red Hen.

Nothing else. Not the slightest movement of the branches. I am never afraid, walking down here in the dark alone. It is a gentle place. I sit on the bench beside the water for a few minutes, and the animals come up and sit beside me, and then we just stay there, companionably, quietly, listening to the water.

Back home, I wonder yet again what book to start reading. I don't feel like one about rivers and streams. And what does that mean – 'feel like'? Books have to slot into a mood, I suppose – or else oppose it.

A new Michael Connelly arrived today but I am saving it for … I have no idea. Just saving it. Proof copies of two more nasty-looking thrillers, way too violent for me, and all about missing children. I am guilty of writing about them, but I would not do it again. Enough already.

I feel thoroughly discontented with every book in the house, until I hit upon Diarmaid MacCulloch. The church historian and Christian commentator, singer in an Oxford choir every Sunday – who is an unbeliever. Strange. But then, I could study the theology of Islam and even become well versed, without believing any of it. Diarmaid writes with great clarity and simple elegance – not true of many theologians. I admire Rowan Williams, the former Archbishop of Canterbury, and always tackle his book reviews and try hard with his books … but dear God, his prose is something so clotted as to be impenetrable. He is erudite and widely and deeply read. A thinker. A philosopher. A poet. A man who appreciates literature at many levels. Yet he finds it hard to write a simple sentence. Is it to do with being Welsh? I can't see why.

Back to Diarmaid MacCulloch's *All Things Made New: Writings on the Reformation*. The Reformation is not my favourite period, probably because of having done it to death for A Level History. I don't care. I have no interest. Henry VIII was a thug, the sixteenth century's Saddam Hussein. Every time I visit Walsingham, and go to look at the beautiful arch, all that is left of that great priory, I am saddened once again by the destruction of so much holy magnificence, such prayerful architecture. He was a vandal, no more, no less. All the psychopaths of history who murdered people whose beliefs did not accord with their own first started on their buildings. Holy architecture.

But I know so little. Diarmaid MacCulloch knows so much. I carry his book off to bed, hoping for enlightenment.

————■•◦•■————

IN CAMBRIDGE FOR A COUPLE OF DAYS. I love the town because I have known it for, well, nearly sixty years, and first discovered it before the tourists and cars and shopping malls gave it a major heart attack and then tried to repair it with a botched coronary bypass. I went around on foot and on the back of a boyfriend's scooter. Few tourists, many bicycles, undergraduates in gowns, men stomping back to their colleges wearing muddy rugger shorts, men carrying hockey and lacrosse sticks over their shoulders and the smell of tea urns wafting down the narrow streets. It was all men. The women's colleges were out of town and females in general few and far between.

But I saw its beauty then, and I still see it – the Backs, the view of King's College Chapel from the river, the misty water flowing under the bridges. And the buildings. Those buildings. It has always been more compact and self-contained than Oxford and, in spite of everything, still is. But now you can barely walk down the pavement because of the gangs of tourists, there is nowhere to park, the streets are choked with traffic and traffic fumes and, of course, the bicycles, still the bicycles.

Apart from the architecture and the river, the best of Cambridge is its bookshops, large and medium, but not small. There is a lot to be said for a small bookshop, but Heffers is iconic. I have never come out of there without having bought too much. Which makes me realise that, setting aside supermarkets for groceries and essential household supplies, bookshops are virtually the only bricks and mortar shops I ever shop in now. Everything is done online. So are some books, come to that. But though I can easily walk straight past every other kind, I cannot resist a bookshop. Small. Medium. Large. Gigantic. The best are those in which are set before you treasures you might never have found – books from very small publishers, and the less obvious new titles from the big ones, who are busy hyping something else. And shelf after shelf of 'backlist' titles – if you want to find all the books in print by, say, P. D. James or Elizabeth Bowen, there they will be, neatly arrayed.

Small bookshops are different. There will be – or should be – a table of the latest bestsellers, but otherwise the stock bears the mark of the proprietor's own taste. I like that.

Cambridge was humming. Full term, smoky sky, mist over the river, playing fields alive with football and rugby and lacrosse players like Brueghel figures in the golden late afternoon. I took my two carrier bags of books happily back to the car. Unpacking those is so much more exciting than unpacking the groceries, if only because I will have forgotten what I bought by the time I get home.

———•○•———

I GOT INTO TROUBLE once for criticising some small independent bookshops. Naturally, every owner, omitting to read the article with care, jumped to the conclusion that I was damning all of them, and theirs in particular. I certainly was not, but the reaction made me realise not only how touchy and defensive people can be, but how paranoid.

I was actually talking about the moribund small bookshops where those working behind the counter have clearly lost the will to live. The stock is uninteresting, the displays more so, and the whole place has an air of those dolls' houses consigned to attics and abandoned there because the children who played with them have grown up.

A few years later, most of those bookshops have closed down, unable to compete with the high street chains. Good. That has made room for some bright, welcoming, lively new ones, full of children reading on bean bags and people having coffee in corners, with handwritten cards stuck to the shelves enthusing about this or that book. 'Recommended by Annie, who wants everyone to read it. A beautiful and moving novel.' That sort of thing.

There is one other off-putting thing still found, and that is a hushed and reverential silence. I am against musak in general but pro it, provided it is at a low level and appropriate, in bookshops. One day, I was in a country bookshop where they were playing a recording of Schubert's Trout Quintet and I said I wished they would not. So they turned it off. The whole place sank into gloom and unease. It was as if we were in an abandoned church. They were right. The place woke up the moment they turned the music back on again. I have seen mothers with small children start to enter a bookshop, only to retreat at either a glare from someone behind the counter or the off-putting hush. These are shops, not monastic chapels or reference libraries for scholars.

Things have improved greatly. They have had to. And as for the people who hate coffee and cake corners in bookshops … I simply do not understand them.

———•○•———

AT LAST THE LEAVES have started to twirl down from the trees and it is looking a lot like autumn. Snow is reported by a friend in Sheffield. Mike, the taxi man, who was born and bred and has lived within a mile of Kings Lynn all of his sixty-two years, says that there will be a frost. He was almost right but around three in the morning, a wind got up, clouds blew over and the thermometer rose.

Whenever the moon and stars are set,
Whenever the wind is high,
All night long in the dark and wet,
A man goes riding by.

(Who else would that be by but Robert Louis Stevenson? He was the best writer of poems for children until Charles Causley and Ted Hughes came along.) That haunted me in my childhood, along with

If you wake at midnight, and hear a horse's feet.
Don't go drawing back the blind, or looking in the street,
Them that asks no questions isn't told a lie.
So watch the wall, my darling, while the Gentlemen go by.

This poem, by Rudyard Kipling, is about smugglers, and why they are so romantic and fascinating and mysterious and delightful. Around the age of nine, I read as many stories about them as I could lay my hands on. I dreamed of joining them, as I also dreamed of running away to the circus. I had no real idea what smugglers and smuggling had really been like. It was a rough trade. But it seemed then, and still seems, a romantic trade, and one which only hurt the Exchequer.

Robin Hood was a hero, too, we believed, robbing the rich to give to the poor. Technically that was, and is, immoral, as well as illegal, and possibly the rich suffered more than the Treasury. Possibly. I think we were all secretly on the side of the law-breakers, though, and sided with them as the authors of the stories did.

There is no modern equivalent. Captain Marryat's *The Children of the New Forest* made Cavaliers of us all. What is there now to rival that romantically persuasive book? I am a sort-of monarchist, so I suppose I must have been a Cavalier in another life. But there is a lot to be said for the Roundheads, morally speaking.

When I started out as a book reviewer, to make enough to pay the rent and the grocery bill while I was writing novels, I was captivated by the story of the Battle of Edgehill and the Verney family. Edgehill was not far from where I lived then. I drove over one November afternoon. It was bitterly cold. I walked from the car to the site of the battle – more or less. I stood there as the sun set and the western sky flushed scarlet and blood red. And I had a terrible, and terrifying, sense of the battle all around me, of the dead and dying men, the terrified, whinnying, rearing horses, the chaos, the smell of death. People say that Edgehill is haunted. Perhaps this is what they mean. Perhaps more. But it was not a good place to be, alone as darkness drew in around me.

As a writer, my imagination seared forever by the novels of Dickens and Thomas Hardy, I depend upon the sense of place. On weather. On the natural world around me. It is the pathetic fallacy, I suppose, to which I am subscribing, without accepting that it is in any way fallacious.

I wonder if *The Children of the New Forest* would be readable now? There is a copy here, among the 'children's classics'. I put that in inverted commas because so many of them were written for adults and inexplicably were thought to have become adopted as favourites by the young. Publishers go on reprinting, re-designing, re-jacketing those titles no child ever reads now. How many editions of *Robinson Crusoe* is it possible to buy? And of *Treasure Island*. The Robert Louis Stevenson just slips under the net, as I have known a few under-twelves to enjoy it, myself among them. But that was sixty-five years ago. Never hand a child today a 'classic' you vaguely assume they will like because you and/or your parents and grandparents did and because it has the word somewhere on the cover.

———•◦•———

SNOW IN YORKSHIRE. Snow forecast nearer here. I hope we are going to get a hard winter. Today the advice of those non-medics employed to nanny us is for the over 65s to keep warm in cold weather, by eating hot meals and drinking hot drinks and wrapping up. I wonder if they ever sit back and ask themselves to whom they are talking? Those of us who lived through the years before central heating, who were not sent out in the morning without having eaten a bowl of porridge, who wore liberty bodices, for Heaven's sake, and a vest and a school shirt and a cardigan and a coat with a lining and long socks inside boots and … Meanwhile, I sometimes pass school bus stops on bitterly cold mornings and see all the teenagers waiting to be transported to school, without coats and the girls in skirts reaching only to their thighs, hatless, bootless …

And now, after a bright sunny start to the day, sleet is battering the window panes.

———•◦•———

WRITERS ARE ASKED the same questions over and over again and a regular one is, 'Do you put real people into your books?' The answer, of course, varies but most would say, 'No' and then, 'Yes.' It is the random detail that finds its way into the fiction. I see someone with an oddly shaped nose, someone very pale, someone with a long horse-like face, or hear someone speaking in a particular way, someone who always wears a hat, someone who always carries whatever they need for the day in a plastic shopping bag. Real people. But probably not recognisable by anyone reading my books, and whose names and life stories are unknown to me.

Otherwise, the usual answer is, 'No.' I think some people want to be 'put into a book'. Certainly, some people are sure that they have been and authors have been sued as a result. But I think it would be very difficult indeed to put a real, living person into a novel, whole and unchanged. There is only so much one knows. The rest is guess work, and how can one know the guesses are correct?

The exception is the novel which is about real characters in history, but the same applies. If I put, say, Virginia Woolf into a book, as Michael Cunningham did in *The Hours*, that Virginia Woolf is not the real one, or only partly. What would she have thought about the picture of herself in that novel? She would have found the exercise interesting and I certainly do not think she would have disapproved, because she knew how it all works and she was all for experiment. But she would probably have said that she was not really like that, or that there was far more to it, or …

The Hours is a clever, carefully designed book. It interested and intrigued me because Virginia Woolf has been my passion and my literary heroine for sixty years. But that Virginia is not altogether my Virginia. Which doesn't matter a jot.

And today, I read that a scholar who has written a new biography of Robert Louis Stevenson has discovered the identity of the real man who inspired, or was the model for, Dr Jekyll/Mr Hyde. RLS had an Edinburgh drinking companion called Eugene

Chantrelle and in some notes he made Stevenson wrote that 'I should say that … Chantrelle bore upon his brow the most open marks of criminality; or rather, I should say so if I had not met another man who was his exact counterpart in looks, and who was yet, by all that I could learn of him, a model of kindness and good conduct.'

Chantrelle murdered his wife by giving her an overdose of opium, and was thought to have killed several others, at supper parties for which he prepared a course of toasted cheese and opium.

The chances are that the identification is correct, and Stevenson was indeed thinking of Chantrelle when he wrote his brilliant novella. But isn't it 'so what'? Chantrelle was clearly one of those psychopathic murderers who had a charming and even an intelligent and erudite side. It is a known profile. I once met a woman who had been a patient of Dr Harold Shipman, when she was a young married woman with small children. She said he had been as patient, gentle and thoughtful a doctor as she could have wished to meet and had looked after her through her pregnancies, and her children through all their various ailments, extremely well. And yet at exactly that time he was in the middle of his murdering career, killing dozens of patients. Of course, his victims all had one thing in common – they were older people, mostly in their seventies and eighties. He posed no threat whatsoever to young women with children, and so my friend always met Dr Jekyll and never, thank God, his alter ego – even though, ominously to my mind, she and he did live in Hyde.

————◆•○•◆————

IF YOU ARE ASKED the same question often enough you begin to wonder if your usual answer is, in fact, the correct one. Why did I write *The Woman in Black*? Why have I gone on writing ghost stories? Do I like to frighten readers? Do I believe in ghosts? Have I ever seen a ghost? And so on.

It is the first two that I need to think about again. I always answer that I had loved ghost stories for many years and that I felt it a pity that it seemed to be, if not a dying, then certainly a 'fading' genre. That most ghost stories are short stories, though two of the best ever written, *A Christmas Carol* and Henry James's *The Turn of the Screw*, are novella length – whatever that is, but under 70,000 words anyway. I wanted to see if I could write one of similar length. All that is true, I think, but at the back of my mind is the thought that there is more. There has to be. I just don't know what it is.

Writers are always asked where they 'get their inspiration from' and usually there is no answer. It just comes. Ideas are nowhere one minute and in one's head the next. Occasionally, I can do better than that. I know what inspired me to write about the First World War – it had been an obsession since my childhood, when I visited my grandmother and great aunts. There were seven of them – though I only knew five – and they had one brother, Sidney, who was killed on his nineteenth birthday, at the Battle of the Somme. There was a photograph of him. The aunts talked about him sometimes. I was aware of the air of sadness, like a wraith among these women, all the time. So began my interest, which became an obsession. I went to the first performance of Benjamin Britten's *War Requiem* in Coventry Cathedral in 1962, after which my obsession continued and increased. I began to read everything I could about 1914–18, but although I wanted to write about it myself, it took me another eight years to pluck up the courage and feel ready.

None of that story has ever changed because it is all very straightforward and I remember the whole thing so clearly. But *The Woman in Black* – written eight or nine years after *Strange Meeting* – is different. I have always said I just do not know where the story, or Eel Marsh House at the end of the causeway, or the small market town of Crythin Gifford, or the woman herself come from. Yet I have that slight sense of their having come from *somewhere* and of knowing where. Yet I don't. The isolated old house is a familiar – some might say essential – ingredient of the ghost story, or indeed any supernatural tale. But the causeway? The death of the child? The young solicitor and his older self, the townspeople who are so strangely silent on the subject of a woman in black who is sometimes seen, with terrible consequences? Where do all these things come from? Out of many novels read and which made an impression, over many years. Out of real places, once visited, not fully recalled and changed into fictional ones. All of those things, I suppose. It is like the ingredients in some recipe, put in and then left to marinade or to steep, until the flavours blend and change and the whole dish becomes more than the sum of its parts. A mysterious business. Best not to delve too deeply into its nature, perhaps. But people go on asking the questions and I go on having to give some sort of answers.

———◦———

THERE IS AN OLD HOUSE right out on the Point, which you can see on clear days and which vanishes in any sea fret or summer morning mist. It stands alone, and I thought it was derelict but apparently it is possible to stay in it, though there is no running water or electricity or sanitation or – well, anything. There is just the sea, the marshes, the sky and the sound the wind and the birds make. I wonder if I dare go?

———•O•———

A FACEBOOK FRIEND asks what his 6-year-old daughter should read next. She has finished *The Magic Faraway Tree* stories. Is she too old for *My Naughty Little Sister*? She has turned up her nose at the Moomins. (What kind of a child is that?) I suggest our old favourite, *Tales of Polly and the Hungry Wolf*. Polly is the Alice in Wonderland of the twentieth century, pert, knowing, and a tiny bit irritating – there are times when one rather wants the wolf to outwit her. It is such an original concept, and so wittily carried out. Lila, at five, loves having the stories read to her, but some of the ironies and word games and general Polly cleverness pass her by just yet. Six will be perfect. Or sixty-six. Anything-six. All the best children's books are enjoyed just as well by adults. That is not true of all the most popular ones. Mind, I defy any adult to stand more than a page of *Diary of a Wimpy Kid* – which is not to descry the books, because they do that magic trick, they get children reading, voraciously. So does Jacqueline Wilson, so does David Walliams. So did, and still does, Roald Dahl. But Dahl, especially *Fantastic Mr Fox*, is to the taste of at least some adults.

Roald Dahl had a gyspy caravan in which to write. I had a shepherd's hut, but left it behind in the Cotswolds. A summerhouse went along with this Norfolk house and at first I thought it would be perfect as my new writing shed. It is not. It is the right building in the wrong place – too far from the house when you have to go back for something vital, like a different pen, or the loo, and across some very rough and often boggy ground. It faces south, which sounds lovely but at any time from late April to October it is likely to be in direct sunlight and boiling. So it is little used. I keep planning a different shed, nearer to the house, facing west, but I am really perfectly happy inside – I move from room to room, at whim.

――――●•○•●――――

A GREAT SKEIN of pink-footed geese went over tonight, in a perfect arrow. How do they choose their leader?

――――●•○•●――――

THE CHRISTMAS LIGHTS switch-on. Always fun, always too early. The lights themselves are hideous, as they all are now, because they are the starry bright white halogen sort, and do that insane chasing round and round. What with that and the electric blue ones, it's enough to give anyone a migraine and epilepsy combined. The churches' lights are always pretty, though, softer, slightly golden – and theirs stay still.

――――●•○•●――――

THE ANNUAL BOOKS OF THE YEAR choices come in and I forgot to do mine for the *Spectator*. I never choose fiction. This year it must be Christopher de Hamel's *Meetings with Remarkable Manuscripts* – such a sumptuous volume but with serious meat on its bones, about medieval 'books'.

I am assembling quite a pile to read over Christmas. Some new, or new to me, plenty read before. V. S. Naipaul's *A House for Mr*

Biswas is slowly becoming my 'novel of all time'. I need a new copy, the old one is now shedding leaves. How touching that book is, how sad and funny. Mr Biswas is a tragic hero. It is really about pride, I think, in the right sense. Pride and family.

DECEMBER

I HAVE PUT OUT the bird feeders again. This long-drawn-out golden autumn meant there were so many berries and seed heads, as well as all the windfalls in the orchard, that they didn't need peanuts and fat balls. The blackbirds and thrushes still forage happily among the juice apples in the long grass, but tits and finches are less well fed – though the teasel heads are covered in tiny birds. I have discovered that buying three big plastic buckets of fat balls at a time on the internet brings the price down and I get free delivery. I would support local shops if it did not cost the same for just one bucket from them *and* I have to lug it home.

The woodburner is lit and the wood pile has been broached. I must be careful with that. Wasps lurk silently inside it and then emerge into the warmth. Yesterday two large hornets flew insolently around the room, getting their bearings. So now a can of Raid, and my emergency EpiPen, are on a sitting room table within reach and I have to wear the fire glove to pick the logs out.

My last blood test apparently showed much lower levels of the specific Ig antibodies – but having almost died of anaphylaxis, I do not feel inclined to rely on the information.

❖

NO ONE GAVE ME a copy of last year's bestseller, Lars Mytting's

Norwegian Wood: Chopping, Stacking, and Drying Wood the Scandinavian Way, so I guess the wood gets stacked the way I like it.

Strange how people give one another random books they are never actually going to read. Thirty-plus years ago, a TV advert for Yellow Pages had a man reading *Fly Fishing* by J. R. Hartley – a book that did not actually exist. It soon did, though, once a publisher clocked that people were asking for it in bookshops. He made a tidy sum out of it for a year. Clever.

Then came books of answers to dotty questions like *How do Armadillos Poo*, or some such. They annoy me, these non-books, not because there is anything actually wrong with them per se, so much as because people will spend some of their limited funds on them to the exclusion of real books – good fiction, great children's books, the best biographies, natural history – anything, really.

———•○•———

DESERTED BEACH TO WALK POPPY on this morning. Dogs are banned here between April and October, so it was an extra pleasure. Huge swathes of golden flat sand. Sea far out. Lifeboat having some paintwork and repairs done. Cheerful men. Cromer pier is deserted, too. Not cold at all, though blowy, which it should be, beside the seaside. Everywhere is in wraps for the winter – candy floss stalls, tea cup rides, playground. Still plenty of fish and chips and ice cream, though. How we longed for 'out of season' when I was growing up in Scarborough. None of these places have ever, or could ever, survive without the summer visitors – and now the weekenders, half-termers, etc., and they are welcome because they keep the towns alive. All the same, to walk on an empty beach on a bright morning – not to mention being able to park close by – is why the rest of us live here all year round.

I walk past the huge Hotel de Paris. In its day it was one of the smart places to holiday – like the Grand Hotel, Scarborough, where Winston Churchill used to stay during Conservative party conferences, and I saw him on its steps – twice.

The Hotel de Paris boasts Oscar Wilde and 'Bosie'. I have never quite bought into the Saint Oscar stuff, but one would go a long way to find a wittier playwright. His stories are good, too – he knew how to shape them. He was a craftsman. Any aspiring writer – any writer, indeed – should be made to read *The Picture of Dorian Grey* and study the way *The Importance of Being Earnest* and *Lady Windermere's Fan* are constructed. OK, so then you are at liberty to ignore it all and do the opposite. But you cannot understand how not to do it until you have first studied how *to*. That is why architects who end up designing buildings shaped like eggs, or aubergines or waves, first learn about angles and planes and weight-bearing loads and straight walls.

THE BLACKBIRDS HAVE STILL NOT FINISHED munching their way through the windfall apples. The robin bobs along the top of the wall, in defiance of the cat. And so many of the leaves hang on and still it is mild. I half expect the hirundines to return and start building under the eaves again.

The swans came on to the pond for half a day. They stay very still, upturned meringues, and hiss fiercely if you go too near. But it is the dog not the people they want to frighten.

Starry night skies, which can be so stunning here, have been sulking behind low cloud and mist. But it is quiet weather. One waits for some cataclysm. They rarely come, but when they do …

There are some parts of the planet man really should not inhabit and New Zealand seems to be one. How can people live under the shadow of an earthquake all the time? And they happen. It isn't like the volcanoes that never erupt. Never say never.

———•○•———

'COLD DECEMBER'S BARENESS everywhere!' as Shakespeare says in Sonnet 97.

Meanwhile, the Christmas requests have started to come in. Elder daughter is first off the mark, as usual, with a list as long as your arm. Younger one will be ages yet, but when hers does come, among the fripperies, I will read, 'Books you think I would like.' I ask you.

———•○•———

FOG. SEA MIST. Sea fret. Different names for much the same thing. And wherever the sea is, the adjacent land will have one hovering about many times a year, especially in winter. Today, I walked out at Blakeney. A fret was swirling about but not settling. There was a mass of thin white cloud with, above that, blue sky and, above that, more misty cloud. And then the sun came striking through and more geese than I have ever seen at one time were suddenly arrowing high up in the blue. Four, five great flocks of them, turning and re-forming, dropping down, soaring up, but always in their arrow shape. After a few moments, they re-assembled and flew lower and directly overhead, making a loud racket.

It was a bit like the RAF, who fly their Tornadoes from nearby. It struck me that both geese and planes accommodate one another in the skies of Norfolk – mostly. A collision between them would be catastrophic for both parties. It happened one winter night when a USAF helicopter flew very low over Salthouse Marshes and disturbed hundreds of resting geese, which rose as one, cannoning into the helicopter and bringing it down with the loss of four lives, as well as of many geese. There was a change to the rules for helicopter flying after that.

———•○•———

HERON ALL OVER THE MUDFLATS. I counted seven, which is most unusual as they tend to be solitary birds, still as statues, waiting patiently, ever watchful. But these were pottering about. Were they herons?

It was very cold.

Came home to light the wood burner and read Hugh Aldersey-Williams's biography of the great eighteenth-century scientist Sir Thomas Browne.

———•○•———

ASKED TO PROVIDE 250 WORDS for Foyles' Christmas promotion on which books I would like to both give and receive this year. Difficult. I spend a lot of my time clearing out unwanted books to make room for the stream coming in. But those are what I call 'disposables' – the best, most handsome books stay, even though some of those have been sent to the charity bookshop recently. I am never again going to spend an evening turning the pages of a huge tome about Rembrandt, or read the 3-volume biography of the nineteenth-century landscape painter Samuel Palmer, beautifully produced though both of these are.

Still, anything to help a bookshop, and books I can give is easier. Jack, the son-in-law, was always easily pleased as he regularly asked for the latest Terry Pratchett – alas. Otherwise, anything new by Andy McNab. After that, he is difficult. He is slightly dyslexic, and he is a musician. He has no heroes or – dread word – hobbies, but he is an excellent cook, of an obsessive and unusual kind, so I will dig about among the new books to find one that covers weird ways of cooking a whole leg of pork or a 15lb piece of best organic beef.

Various children are taken care of with the latest Jacqueline Wilson/David Walliams/anything about dinosaurs. It's sounding dull. I want to give everyone something that will wake them up – but the risk is that they won't like it.

Pity dogs and cats don't read.

———•◦•———

IN THIS, THE PEAK SEASON for non-books, even the museums and galleries are on to them, but the British Library has had the originality to design and publish a series of books people might actually want to read. Their growing list of 1930s/1940s/1950s classic crime novels, with some of the best covers I have seen for many a day, is so well chosen. I bought half a dozen when I went into the bookshop to get a copy of the new David Walliams story for a child. Freeman Wills Croft. Anthony Berkeley. Writers of those vintage, well-made, tightly plotted detective novels set on ocean liners, in vicarages and country inns and stately homes and smart old-fashioned hotels and Oxbridge colleges. Characters are pasteboard, narrative line and scene-setting are all. Some are much better than others, but they all serve to divert one for a couple of days in bed with a bad cold.

Meanwhile, the rest either have coffee table books about their own collections – Greek vases and statues, exhibitions of fashion designers, illuminated manuscripts which weigh a ton and cost a fortune, or else small facsimile books – 'Navigational Instructions for Spitfire Pilots', 'The Workings of the V2 Bomber', 'Parachuting for Recruits', that sort of thing. And then there are the nostalgia books. The things we knew – 'Thirty Days Hath September', 'Times Tables', 'Collective Nouns', 'French Conjugations', 'Recipes from the 1940s WI' …

There is no end in sight for these, so long as someone has an archive they can plunder. They come and go, they have their day, everyone gets at least one at Christmas, after which they are dead as dodos again.

They are really upmarket stocking fillers, bought by people who disdain wind-up grannies on mobility buggies and plastic nuns who do the splits. And rude things. It is a book. It will improve you/occupy your mind, or at least Take You Back.

Harmless, of course. But somehow they still annoy me. All except those British Library detective novels.

———•○•———

HAVING DISMISSED ALL THE NON-BOOKS, of course I bought one this morning. The new series of Enid Blyton's Famous Five books are non-books but clever and funny. So probably not non-books. Whatever. I bought three copies of *Five Go Gluten Free* for various GF friends – only one of whom is coeliac and so has a serious medical reason for it.

I also bought last year's new Andy McNab for son-in-law because I think I missed it last year. The new Zadie Smith novel for younger daughter. Roy Strong's latest volume of diaries for the SP – which will be a waste of money because he is sure to have bought it for himself, in that annoying way he has of spending money on everything he likes during the last weeks of December.

———•○•———

TIDE OUT AT BLAKENEY. Very mild. Few birds. Seagulls, of course, but there always used to be masses of over-winterers, until they let the estuary silt up. Waiting to see something very rare. A man came towards me and said in a low voice that on the old gate down there was an arctic finch. I followed his pointing finger to it. Pretty, nervous little bird, but sitting bold as brass on the top strut of the gate, and unmistakeable. No one much was about, but as I crept away I met an army of twitchers, tripods and long lenses over their shoulders, bobble hats on heads, chattering away as they marched. Word had got out. It only takes one text message.

I hoped the little arctic finch flew away – it probably did, the racket they were making. I walked back to the car hugging myself with secret delight that for a moment or two, the quiet man and I had had it all to ourselves.

———•○•———

HAS DONALD TRUMP ever read a book?

———•○•———

CHRISTMAS, LIKE SO MANY OTHER THINGS in life, is all anticipation, that and lists. And money.

But if by today, the 25th, it isn't done, it won't get done. Today is the day to feel the strange tingle that is Christmas. It comes with the sound of the first carol. But even more, for me, the carol as played by a Salvation Army band, in a high street, at a railway station.

There are family Christmas rituals. One man I knew always ate pork pie for Christmas Day breakfast. Another always goes for a swim in the sea. Our children were always allowed to open just one present on Christmas Eve, just before going to bed. It takes the edge off the nausea of over-excitement. It's pot luck, of course. Sometimes the present pile under the tree, dithered and dithered over for ages, the one chosen, put back, chosen again … then, finally, chosen for good … sometimes, it is the best possible one of all. A night light that sends gentle softly coloured pictures moving around the bedroom wall, to soothe to sleep. A pair of new furry slippers with rabbit ears on the front.

But not always. Like the Christmas when the present elder daughter finally settled on turned out to be an umbrella. A *brown* umbrella, and from her godfather of all people. I still believe he wrapped up the wrong item because what godfather with half a brain would give a 5-year-old a brown umbrella for Christmas?

———••○••———

I LOVE HAVING BOOKS that you can only read once a year. When the daughters were small we had a table of only-for-Christmas picture books set out. *Lucy and Tom's Christmas. Christmas at Bullerby*. The Jan Pieńkowski gold and red Christmas pop-up book, *Christmas Kingdom. Thomas and the Christmas Tree* …

I always read the story from St Matthew's Gospel in the Authorised Version on Christmas Eve, and usually think about the characters who only walk on. Who they were. What they thought. How they felt. The innkeeper's wife. One of the shepherds whose young son was left tending the sheep, while they all raced off downhill to Bethlehem. The pages to the Three Kings. Real people? Real people. It is like those who happened to be out in the streets when Jesus was being taken to Golgotha, carrying His cross. Because this seems such a momentous event to us that we think everyone must have been watching, silently. But crucifixions were an everyday occurrence. They would have seen such a man being goaded along often enough. Jesus was well-known, of course. Many had heard him preach and word about his trial and sentence at the hands of Pontius Pilate would have got round. Even so, as it was Passover, people would have been going about their business, busy preparing. Some went to stare at the procession of the man carrying his own cross, but probably not many.

Whatever the truth of the matter, or of who Jesus was, these things happened. And even if the events of the Christmas story, as related, did not, it doesn't matter. It is a powerful fable and a beautiful story, or why else would there be dozens of shepherds and angels and kings and Josephs and Marys dressed from the costume wardrobe, performing the story as a play in hundreds of schools and churches across the country every year. Every year. That is a powerful fable.

After that, I have to re-read A *Christmas Carol*, though I scarcely need to, I know it almost by heart. It is moving, frightening, funny, heart-warming, instructive. It has a moral. It has everything. Dickens got it right. The ghosts of Christmas Past, Present and Future – especially the last – have the power to move and to change us. I don't know of any other book set around the

Christmas season which does that and so memorably – other than the story in the Gospel according to Luke.

——•○•——

BY NOW, THE TURKEY is in a big pot making soup and those who came to stay have probably gone.

Presents hastily unwrapped, thanked for and set aside to be looked at carefully later, sit waiting and there is always, always a pile of new books.

——•○•——

AFTER THE CHRISTMAS GHOST STORIES I am reading, as ever, a classic English detective story – and they are different from crime novels, it isn't just a question of a change or even an update of genre name.

It has to be by Dorothy L. Sayers or Freeman Wills Crofts or Michael Innes or one of their fellows, though I rarely re-read Agatha Christie now. At any rate I like them set in the 1920s and 1930s or just occasionally immediately before the war.

This year it is Marjorie Allingham's masterpiece, *The Tiger in the Smoke*, a dark and sometimes rather frightening book. At its heart is 'the ancient smell of evil, acrid and potent as the stench of fever', in the form of a ruthless murderer, Jack Havoc, and of the albino pack-leader, Tiddy Doll.

This is not a whodunnit but a whydunnit, a complex novel of character, and at its heart, it is also about the essentially Biblical and Miltonian conflict between good and evil. The devil is Jack Havoc and the angel comes in the form of the saintly Canon Avril.

One of the marks of the good novel of any genre is that it bears frequent re-reading, and that it yields more each time. The plot of *The Tiger in the Smoke*, once known, is known for good. It is not the plot that matters on subsequent readings.

If the characters are the best Allingham ever created, there is another character that she was very familiar with and loved, that was not a human being but a city – London. She knew it as Dickens knew it, she walked about its streets and courts and alleyways and beside its great river over many years and she wove its streets and its characters together and they know London as intimately as she knew it. It is a city of light and dark, and the good and evil of men and women are mirrored in the two faces of their city. Canon Avril's vicarage is warm, comfortable and comforting, an oasis of muddled and challenged but still essentially happy family life. And then there is the other London, where a rag-tag street band of ex-soldiers and vagrants live in one bleak cellar, when they are not wandering the streets playing a cacophony of instruments and through which they go in fear of their leader, Tiddy Doll. There are dark side alleys where a man can be trapped and swiftly murdered, the soulless public houses where people meet briefly, and secretly. And over them all, there is the fog, a Dickensian 'London particular', spreading like a stain, insinuating itself into every crack and crevice, muffling and blinding, choking and confusing. The fog is sinister and frightening and anything may happen within it and be concealed – secrets, evil deeds, swift, cunning movements. The fog gets into nostrils and lungs and eyes – and in some strange way, into hearts and minds, too.

The detective in the novel is Albert Campion, who in earlier novels was a cross between Bertie Wooster and Lord Peter Wimsey – chinless, receding hair, posh voice, willowy figure. An irritating man. But here he has changed totally. He is now married with a son, and he has become a man of courage and intelligence and foresight, with a well-trained clever mind, one who energetically assists the police and is appreciated for it. He knows evil when he encounters it. He can sense it. He can smell it. And about Jack Havoc, he is right.

I think *The Tiger in the Smoke* has survived and grown in stature since its original publication – if that can be said to happen with a book. It does so for the same reasons that Dickens survives and reads to us with the freshness it read to its original public. Some compliment for a detective story.

I settled down with it again last evening and was lost in it, and tense from being caught up in it, for hours. What else are winter nights for?

The tawny owl believes they are for sitting on the chimney pot and hooting so that the eerie sound seems to be emanating from within the room itself. We never see it, though, unlike the barn owl, which is so bold in daylight, so close to hand and fearless and familiar.

DULL DAYS NOW, half in half out of Christmas. The town streets full of people mooching *en famille*. They look in shop windows as if they have forgotten that now they have actually finished buying last-minute presents.

This is the time of year for battening down the hatches and getting a lot of work done. Everybody in the media world has forgotten about us writers. They won't wake up and remember us until at least 6 January, so let's leave them dozing and tiptoe away.

ONE OF THE BEST PRESENTS anyone can give you is the name of a writer whose books they believe will be 'you' – and they are. Someone you would almost certainly never have found for yourself. They expand your horizons, they enrich you, they lead you forward, they chime with truths you already know and confirm them, they share new truths of their own with you.

Not being a great reader or explorer of contemporary poetry, I am quite sure I would never have discovered Mary Oliver for myself. She is an American, now in her old age and living in Provincetown, Massachusetts, a Pulitzer Prize-winner. She writes with both eyes, ears and most of her mind focused on the country. She knows natural life intimately, she knows the names of things and their habits and habitats. She loves every living creature. She says that she believes everything has a soul. This sort of thing so often goes towards the making of a bad poet, someone soft and sugary, sentimental and wispy. But there is backbone to Mary Oliver, and she says things she wants you to hear.

There is a beautiful poem, 'Blake Dying', about the poet William Blake, in Oliver's collection *A Thousand Mornings*.

He felt himself growing heavier.
He felt himself growing lighter.

When a man says he hears angels singing,
he hears angels singing.

That stanza, repeated, stressed, tells all:

When a man says he hears angels singing,
he hears angels singing.

Such a writer is always an animal lover and more often a cat lover. She does not say much about cats – though she is keen on foxes. But Mary Oliver is primarily a dog lover. Strange that.

———•◦•———

SOME WORDS, SOME SENTENCES, some names, some stories are part of the fabric of my mind, part of the store of references and images I was certainly not born with but which I began to acquire and memorise as a child and continued to absorb through all my growing up and into adulthood. I heard the Bible being read and the prayers of the Church of England services – the words of Morning Prayer, the Eucharist and Evensong, the Collects – all from *The Book of Common Prayer* and the hymns from *The English Hymnal.* I am still surprised at how much I know of all this by heart, and I was not from a vicarage family. I wasn't alone. Everyone used to know chunks of the Bible because they heard it without fail every Sunday, and those who could not read it did not really need to, they listened and remembered over the years.

I did Latin at school, and Greek for a couple of years later, but the Classical stories were told to us and read to us in English, so they too became part of my frame of cultural reference. Folk tales, fairy stories, great poetry are in there, too. It was not anything out of the way. We all knew these things. It was what happened in school and out of it.

It makes me sad that the Bible, the Prayer Book, the Classical canon are not part of my own children's fabric. The rot set in forty years ago or more. I doubt if they know anything much by heart and it is not their fault. Schools regard learning by rote as time-wasting and sterile and how does a rich store of literary and cultural references help one in Real Life?

The Collects are a particular source of beautiful cadences and deep meaning. They are inspiring, and comforting, and they are all quite short, so reading the Collect of the Day each morning takes only a couple of minutes.

You need not be a believer to gain a lot. This reading is a form of meditation and mindfulness and, goodness knows, those are all the rage. I think the Collects strengthen one's mental immune system and guard against all manner of ills. Is that just me?

O God,
you know us to be set
in the midst of so many and great dangers,
that by reason of the frailty of our nature
we cannot always stand upright:
grant to us such strength and protection
as may support us in all dangers
and carry us through all temptations;
through Jesus Christ your Son our Lord.

———•○•———

HAVE ALWAYS WONDERED why my antipathy to William Wordsworth is so ingrained. Then today I wondered if it was because of his intensely political spell – unless you are a historian, and more, a political historian, the passions of the political past do not heat up well. Even those poets and other artists who marched off to fight in the Spanish Civil War are of interest now because of their poetry. Politics is such a fleeting thing.

I never got Wordsworth at all. Nor the overblown Keats. But Coleridge, now ... there is that streak of lightning in him, genius, which makes Wordsworth seem so leaden.

> *Through caverns measureless to man.*
> *Down to a sunless sea.*

And the desperation of the Ancient Mariner, Kubla Khan and all the rest that blazed out of that opium-fuelled imagination.

> *... Beware! Beware!*
> *His flashing eyes, his floating hair!*
> *Weave a circle round him thrice,*
> *And close your eyes with holy dread*
> *For he on honey-dew hath fed,*
> *And drunk the milk of Paradise.*

Makes flames come out of your ears.

———◦———

I WAS TRYING TO THINK of lines, or passages, that shock the reader into crying out, 'Oh NO!' A bit like the second when the identity of the killer is at last revealed in Agatha Christie's *The Murder of Roger Ackroyd*. I first read it on a long train journey, and jumped when I got to that bit and did indeed shout, 'Oh NO!'

The traveller opposite smiled. 'Good, isn't it?' he said.

But it is another sort of shock, one of disbelief and immense sadness, when one reaches the Time Passes section of Virginia Woolf's *To the Lighthouse*.

Mr Ramsay, stumbling along a passage one dark morning, stretched his arms out, but Mrs Ramsay having died rather suddenly the night before, his arms, though stretched out, remained empty."

Once you have taken the novel to your heart, and loved Mrs Ramsay, you never get her shocking offstage death out of your mind. Indeed, it is one book which does change after the first reading because you can never un-know what happens, and so, in a strange way, you slightly withhold your affection for her.

The denouement of any crime novel or thriller may give the reader a jolt but one reads those genres precisely in order to be jolted. Virginia Woolf plants her shock carefully and cleverly, to make the maximum impact. It is not for one moment foreseen.

I have tried to do that myself in novels, from time to time. It has succeeded sometimes. And it has not. One plays a dangerous game with the reader.

————◉————

THE BOAT MAKERS AND MENDERS at Glandford are busy repairing, refurbishing and painting all winter. The smell of varnish floats on the air.

News is that there is likely to be a record number of seal pups on the Point. There was a record number last year, too. Seals are thriving.

News also has it that we are going to have a bitterly cold winter, and another Ice Age will start in four years time.

All depends on who you believe.

Looking at the still water under a bright sky this morning, the poem went through my mind about the lonely sea and the sky.

And all I ask is a tall ship and a star to steer her by;

(John Masefield – a better poet than is often thought. Poet Laureate, too. Not to mention author of one of the best children's books, *The Box of Delights*.)

I often wish I had spent time in small boats on the water. I should have done. I am a good sailor, too. Whether you are or you aren't is pure luck. Too late now, so watching will have to do.

———————•◦•————————

READING JAMES WOOD'S *How Fiction Works* again, I am reminded how sane a writer and commentator he is, how balanced and clear-headed and full of common sense: 'The novel is the great virtuoso of exceptionalism: it always wriggles out of the rules thrown around it.'

There *are* no rules, I say over and over again.

'Show, don't tell.' That is one of the worst 'rules' – you do what you want, when writing a novel. Some of the very greatest ones tell, and either never show or only show some of the time. Henry James's *The Portrait of a Lady*. Ford Madox Ford's *The Good Soldier*. V. S. Naipaul's *A House for Mr Biswas* ... They tell and show and the telling sections are there because the author knew they were the best way of writing this or that particular section. James Wood highlights the scene where the author tells how Mr Biswas went on his bicycle to purchase a dolls' house for his daughter, which cost more than a month's wages. 'Not a word of dialogue' and even the key moments are described 'off stage'.

None of the rules are obeyed.

There are no rules.

It would help aspiring authors considerably if they understood that.

————•◦•————

MINUS 4 OUT THERE.

Norfolk night skies are beautiful and there is so little light pollution here it is possible to see the constellations very clearly. I keep trying astronomy. People have bought me books about the night sky, and telescopes and DVDs and … It's no good. Once they take away the dot-to-dot line, it all looks a mess. I can sort out Orion, and the Belt, the Great Bear and the Pleiades and once, I think, I got Bootes and Cassiopeia, but that's it. In summer here you can lie on your back on the grass and see the Milky Way. Parts of our coast get the Northern Lights, but I always hear about it the next day. I would love to go on a Northern Lights trip to the very very far north but I don't suppose I ever shall.

Did anyone ever write a novel about the night sky? SF, I suppose, and I can't get on with SF. As Shakespeare said in *Much Ado about Nothing*:

'[A] *star danced, and under that was I born.*'

That will do.

————•◦•————

MEANWHILE, NEW TELEVISION adaptations of Agatha Christie are announced, and they mean to shock. No gentle Geraldine McEwan as Miss Marple, nor the mincing Hercule Poirot of David Suchet. These will, apparently, be strong stuff, about murder as it really is and murderers ditto. Fast-paced. Violent. I think Christie can take it. And, as ever, if people don't like the new adaptations, the old ones will trundle along in the twilight world that is after-noon television, and of course the books do not change. People forget. When I wrote *Mrs de Winter*, the sequel to *Rebecca*, some people were cross ... and when I pointed out that a) they didn't have to read it, and b) *Rebecca* was still there as it was written by Daphne du M, they missed the points. But no adaptation or sequel or whatever can ever change the original book. Not now. In the eighteenth century Nahum Tate re-wrote *King Lear*, giving it a happy ending and, as if that were not bad enough, he managed to have the original Shakespeare play banned so that only his was played or read. Now, that is a wholly different matter and shocking. That is what fascist dictatorships do with books they do not like.

———•◦•———

I JUST WENT OUTSIDE. It smells of cold and the grass is crisp. Wish I could find the poem I read many years ago, about opening the door at night and just standing, taking in what it is like out there ...

———•◦•———

AND SO, THE LAST DAY of the year. I have never done anything celebratory about it – a non-event if ever there was one. But the last week of December shows two faces. The shortest day has come and gone. By infinitesimal steps, the nights are drawing out. The birds sing again. The rite of excess that Christmas has become is over. There is just the aftermath in terms of family fall-outs and over-indulged children and stomachs.

But January is a new start. There is spring to look forward to. No matter how grim it, and February, may be, if I get my head down and get through them, March comes and in March there really is spring to look forward to.

Yet, today it is still December and the Old Year. Everything is fast in its winter hibernation, like the Moomins under their duvets during the Long Sleep. The fires and stoves are lit. The wood pile is stacked high. Not even a snowdrop has yet dared to struggle towards the light in some sheltered spot.

This is a time for thinking. Reading. More reading. Making writing notes. Reading again. Dreaming. Wondering. Scheming. Planning. Hunkering down. Lighting the lamps.

Settling.

I go outside and have my nose bitten off by cold. The dog and the cat turn their back to the outside world and burrow deep down into their baskets.

Snowflakes drift down from a laden, leaden sky.

I come inside. And close the door.

BOOK LIST